Josiah Pittman, Michael William Balfe, Edward Fitzball

# The Siege of Rochelle

Opera in Two Acts

Josiah Pittman, Michael William Balfe, Edward Fitzball

**The Siege of Rochelle**
*Opera in Two Acts*

ISBN/EAN: 9783337389925

Printed in Europe, USA, Canada, Australia, Japan

Cover: Foto ©Thomas Meinert / pixelio.de

More available books at **www.hansebooks.com**

# THE

# SIEGE OF ROCHELLE:

## 𝔒𝔭𝔢𝔯𝔞

## IN TWO ACTS.

THE MUSIC COMPOSED BY

## BALFE,

## THE WORDS BY E. FITZBALL.

# INDEX.

## ACT I.

# DRAMATIS PERSONÆ.

| | | | |
|---|---|---|---|
| CLARA. | *Soprano.* | MICHEL. | *Tenore or Baritono.* |
| MARCELLA. | *Mezzo Soprano.* | ROSENBERG. | *Basso.* |
| VALMOUR. | *Tenore.* | MONTALBAN. | *Basso.* |
| SCHWARTZ. | *Tenore.* | AZINO. | *Basso.* |

CHORUS—RETAINERS—SOLDIERS—PEASANTS, etc.

*The scene is laid near Rochelle.*

COUNT ROSENBERG, a young and gallant officer in the service and confidence of the Prince Elector, has fallen in love with the Princess Euphemia, the Elector's daughter, and betrayed the Prince's confidence by secretly marrying her. A child, Clara, being born, the Count to screen his own guilt has torn the infant from the bosom of Euphemia and secretly given it into the charge of an adventurer named Montalban, who was then one of his followers. It was supposed the child in charge of Montalban was his own daughter, while those who knew of the Count's secret marriage with Euphemia believed their child to be dead. Clara Montalban, as she was called, when fully grown, was placed by her reputed father in the service of the Marquis de Valmour, a general officer in the French army, to watch over his only son. Clara, however, being possessed of rare beauty, and accomplished manners, so enchanted the Marquis de Valmour, who had now become a widower, that he proposed to marry her, when Montalban, seeing in the child of the first marriage of Valmour an obstacle to the inheritance of the immense fortune of the Marquis, which fortune he hoped would devolve upon Clara and himself were the child removed, determined to murder him. Accordingly, one day Montalban found his way to the garden where Valmour's child was playing, and there slew him. In making his escape however, he was seen and detected by Clara, who was near the spot. When the horrible deed was discovered, Clara was accused of being the perpetrator, she being the only one who had the care of the child, and who could have an interest in committing the crime. She in vain protested her innocence, but her filial feeling would not permit her to accuse her own father. All proofs being against her, she was sentenced to death by the judges, only, through the interference of Count Rosenberg, who knew Clara was his daughter, a commutation of the sentence was obtained from the king, and she was condemned to pass the remainder of her life in a convent on the banks of the Rhine.

Clara, through the connivance of a good monk, Azino, to whom she had confessed her secret, has contrived to escape and take refuge in a farm near Rochelle, where she remained under the name of Olympia, protected by Friar Azino, who was Superior of the Convent of Monks in that vicinity. During this time the fortress of Rochelle was besieged by the Royal French army, and Valmour had been sent by the king to the besieging camp as a general officer. Count Rosenberg also, who had been absent for some time travelling, had returned home, together with his old and faithful servant MICHEL, the owner of the farm wherein Olympia was living, and had resumed his services in the army at the siege of Rochelle. The presence of Valmour having been made known to Clara, she goes to the convent to inform Azino of her perilous situation, and the danger of being discovered, and to invoke his assistance in finding some safer place of abode, but she is there met and recognized, in the presence of Michel and his wife, by Valmour himself who has happened to pass that way. Valmour who has always believed Clara innocent, entreats Marcella and Michel to keep the secret, and begs Clara to fly for safety. As Clara and Azino are on the point of leaving the convent, Rosenberg and Montalban arrive, bringing in wounded soldiers and monks after the attack on the fortress; on recognizing Clara, they proclaim her an object of horror to all near. Under their taunts Clara is almost driven to reveal her secret, and accuse her father, but Montalban threatening her with his malediction, contrives to make her silent, and she flies in despair. Meanwhile, Rosenberg, who believes her guilty, has repudiated her as his daughter, and Montalban, terrified at the idea of Clara accusing him of the murder, is scheming her destruction.

In the Chateau of Euphemia guests and vassals are celebrating the birthday of Euphemia, Count Rosenberg's wife, the Count and Valmour being expected. In the midst of the festivities a cry of help is heard outside, and Clara is discovered in distress with her garments torn. By order of Euphemia she is brought into the hall where she sinks down exhausted. Questioned by Euphemia Clara tells how she has escaped from Rochelle. Michel and Marcella now arrive to announce the approach of Count Rosenberg and Valmour, and are greatly astonished to find Clara there. During the ceremonies Clara is seen crossing the back of the hall attempting to escape, but is recognized by the Count and Marquis and denounced to the Princess as a person unworthy of her compassion. Montalban who has come with Rosenberg is now aware of the presence of Clara, and, in secret, proposes to remove her to the Indies. For this purpose Michel is requested to attend with a boat at night. Montalban watches his opportunity and orders Clara to follow him, but she refuses, saying: " I will not go with the assassin of Valmour's son!" Michel has overheard this and swears to protect the girl. She is seized by Montalban and dragged senseless to the boat, but when nearing the opposite bank Michel purposely capsizes it, and saves Clara by swimming with her to land. She is now placed in a hermitage, and disguised as a Sister of Mercy is conducted to Rochelle. Montalban having escaped drowning now becomes traitor, and being bribed by the Duke of Rohan, he betrays Rosenberg into the hands of the besieged. While Montalban is leading Rosenberg through the fortress, Clara, hidden from sight, overhears their conversation. Rosenberg accuses Montalban of treason and stigmatizes him as a man without honour or conscience. Montalban in his turn asks Rosenberg where his honour and conscience were when he betrayed the Elector's confidence and repudiated his daughter Clara, giving her to him, Montalban. Unable to restrain herself Clara rushes forward and asks Rosenberg if he and not Montalban is her father. On Rosenberg answering, yes! Clara points out Montalban as the assassin of Valmour's child. which revelation she could not make while supposing he was her father. Montalban endeavours to stab Rosenberg but Michel who has been made prisoner interposes in defence of his master. Montalban orders the guard to fire on all the rebels, but at this moment a shell striking the rampart near to Montalban, buries him under the ruins. A rumour of battle is heard, the fortress has been attacked by the besiegers, and Valmour at the head of the victorious army, enters through the breach. He comes to behold Clara justified and declared innocent of the horrible crime of which she had so long been accused.

# OVERTURE.

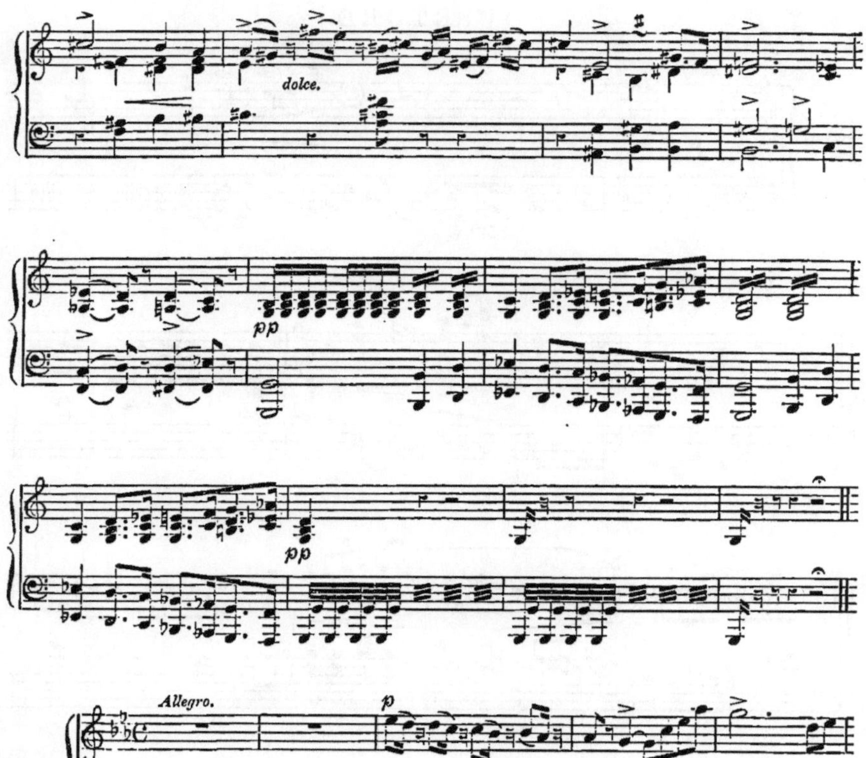
dolce.
pp
pp
Allegro.
PIANO-FORTE.
p
p
f
p
f
p

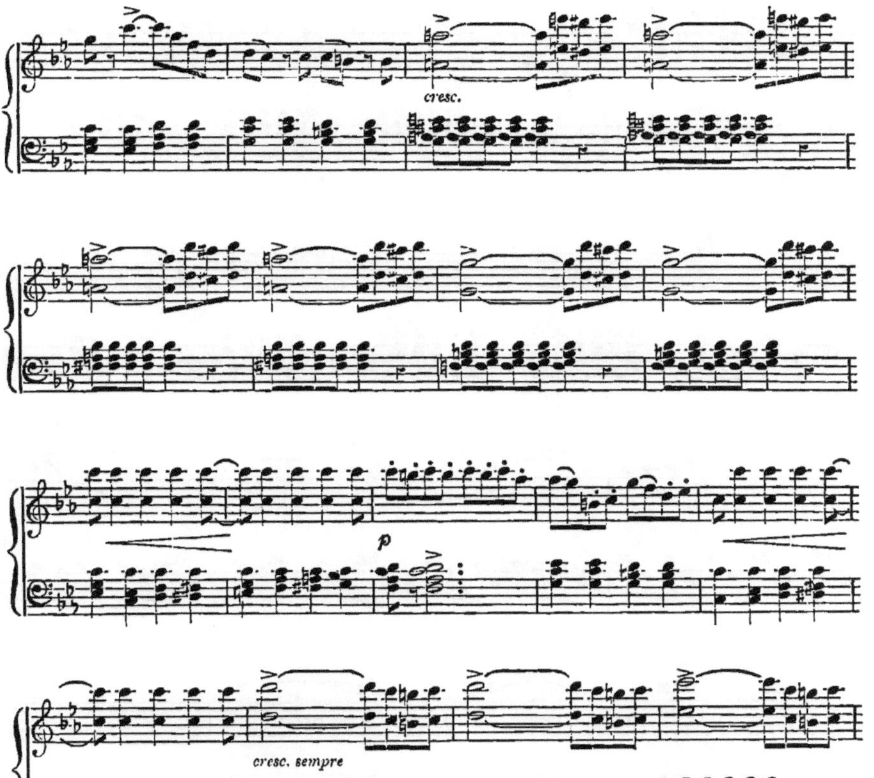
cresc.
p
cresc. sempre
ff
p
ff

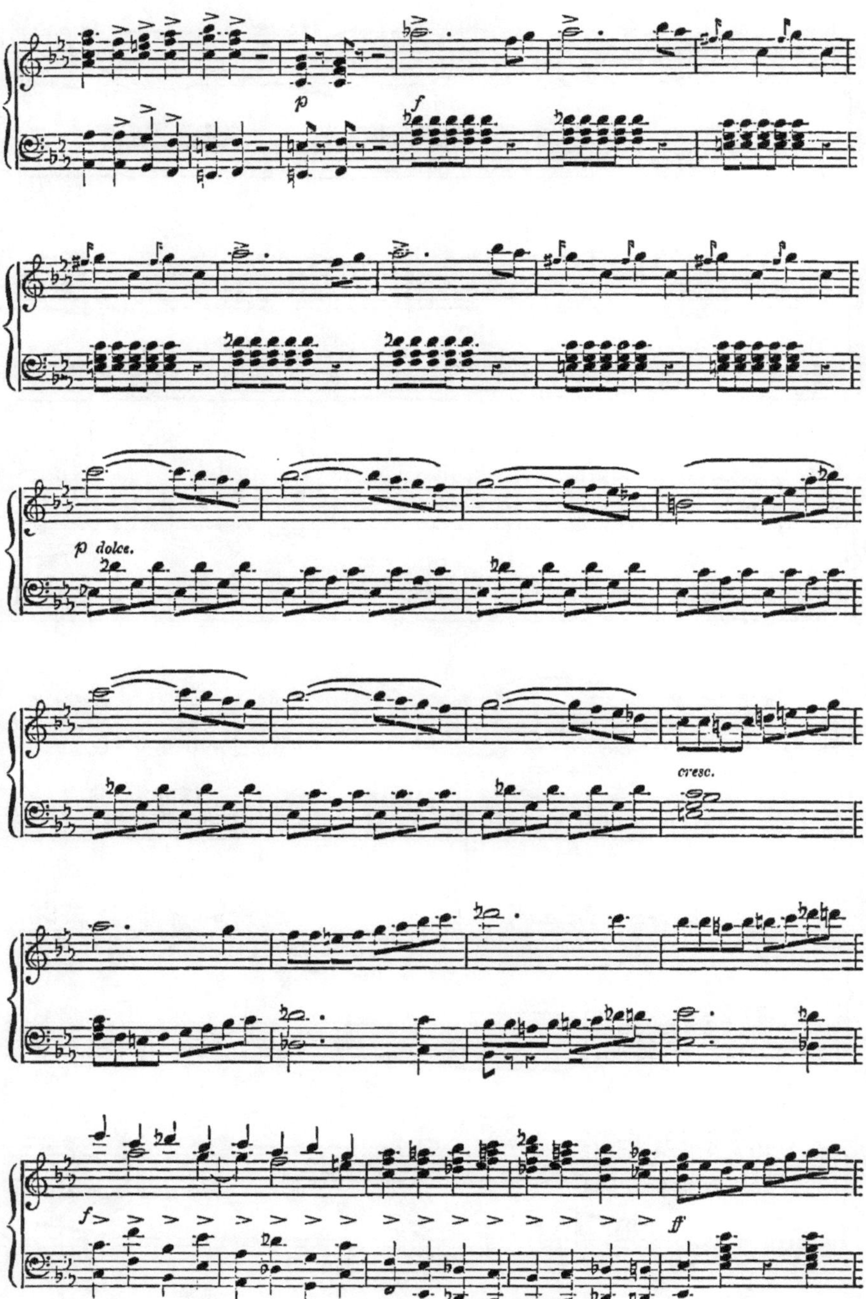
p
f
p dolce.
cresc.
f
ff

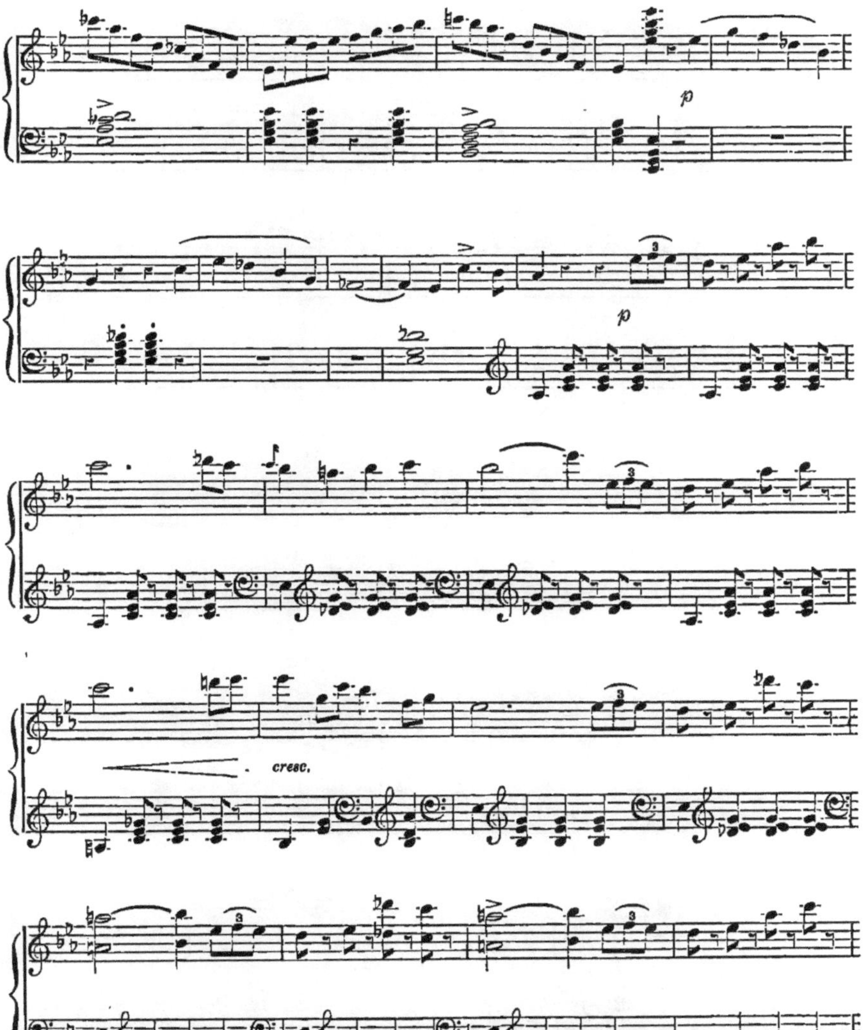
p
p
cresc.
brillante.

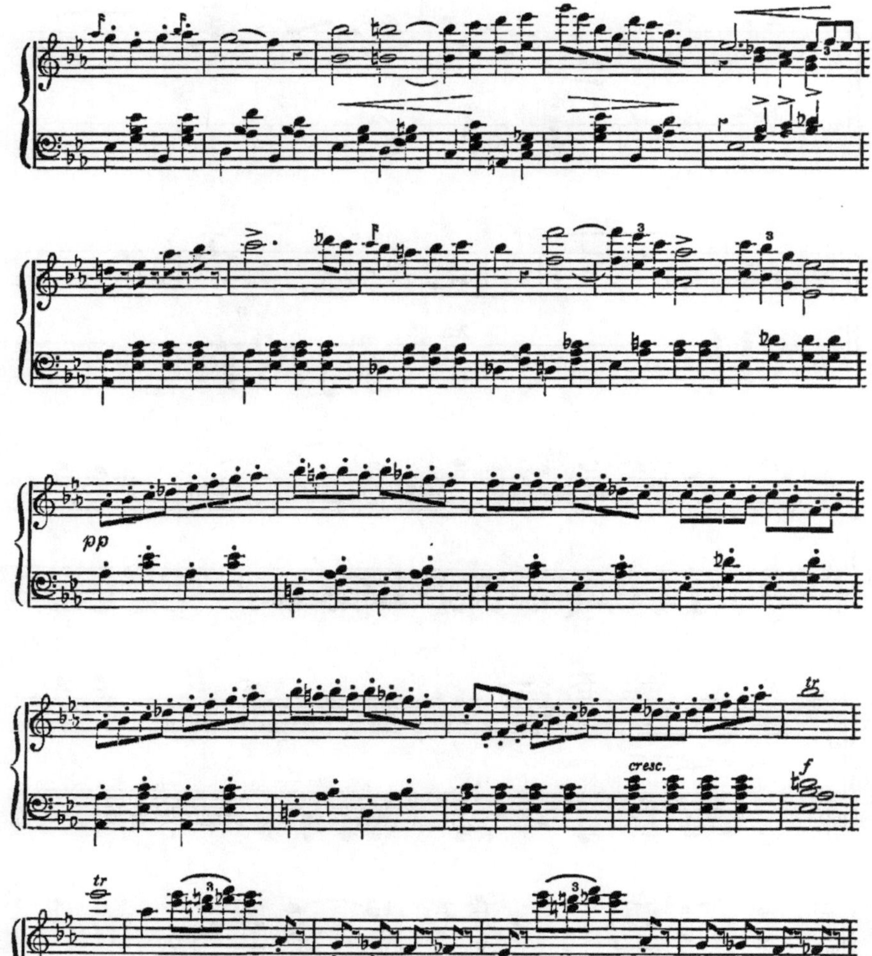
pp
cresc.
f
tr
ff
p

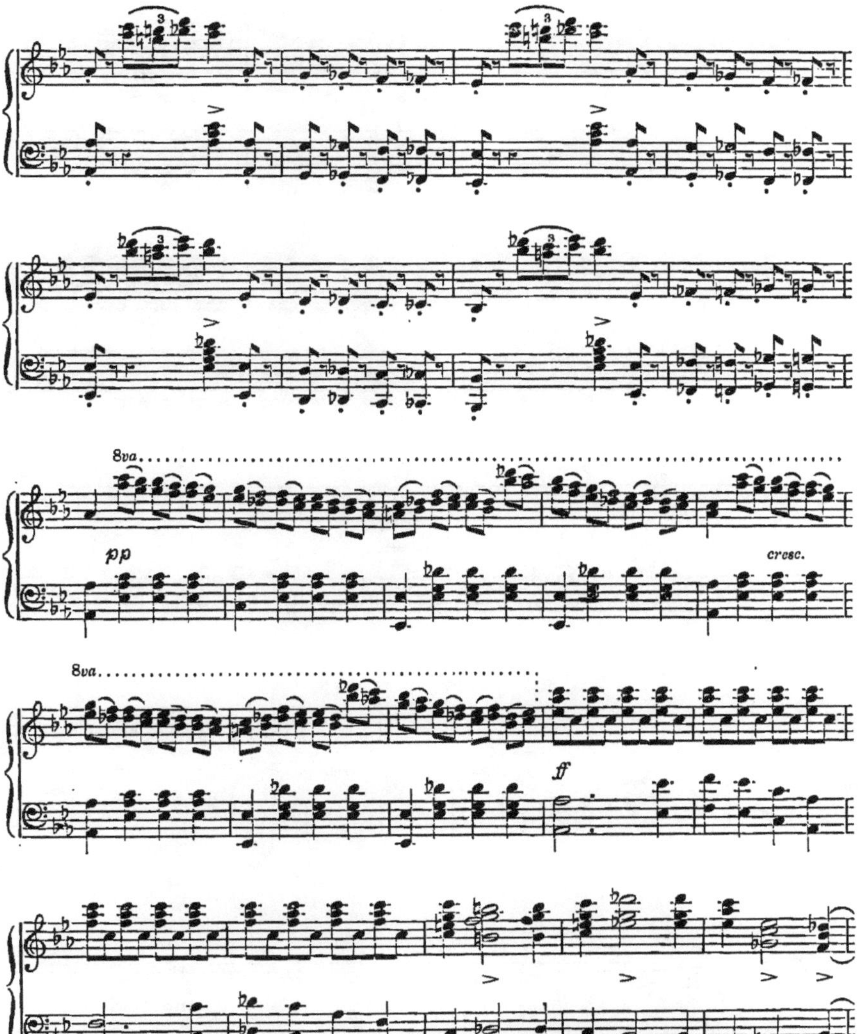
3
3
3
3
8va
pp
cresc.
8va
ff
ff

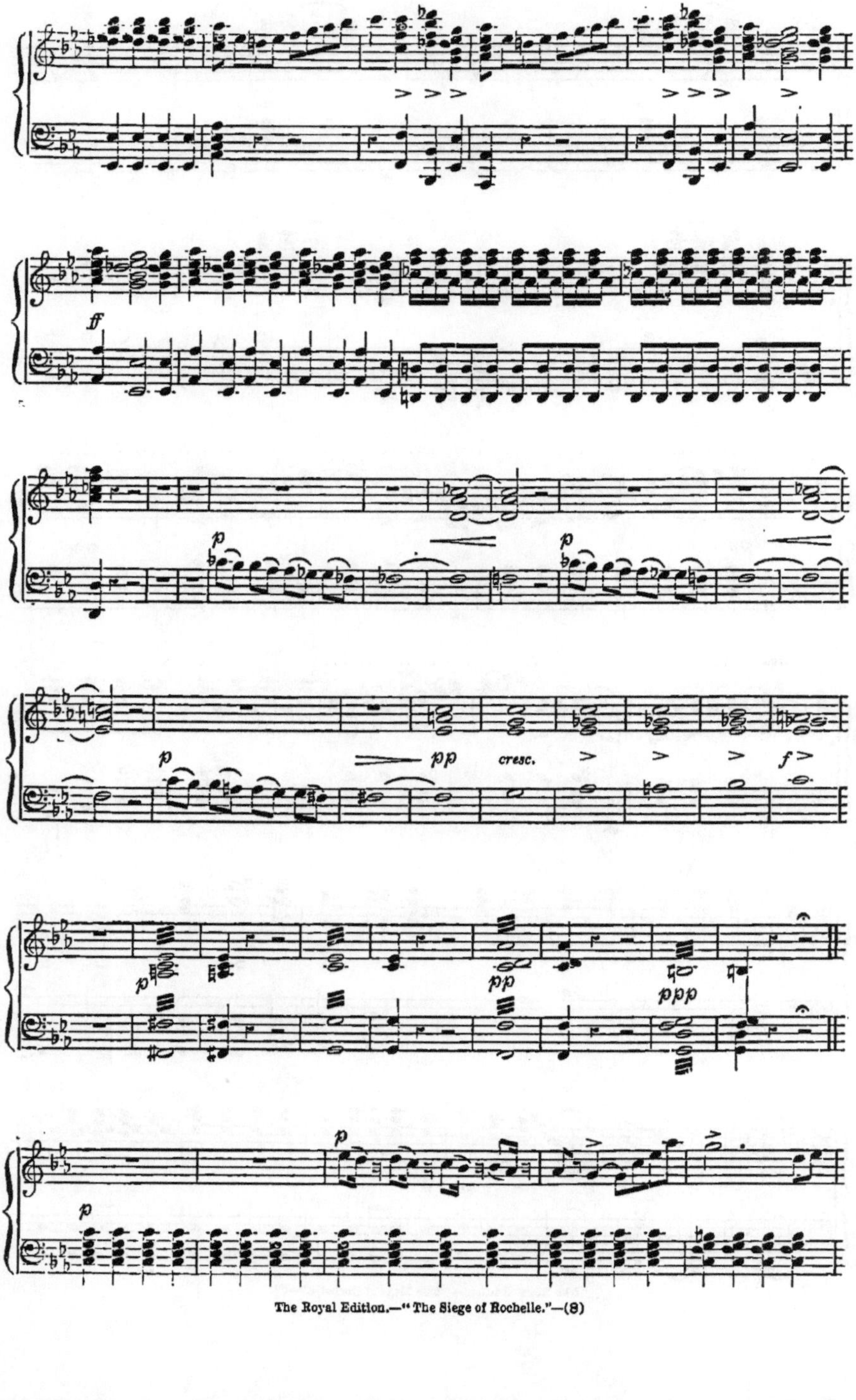
ff
p
p
p
pp
cresc.
f
p
pp
ppp
p
p

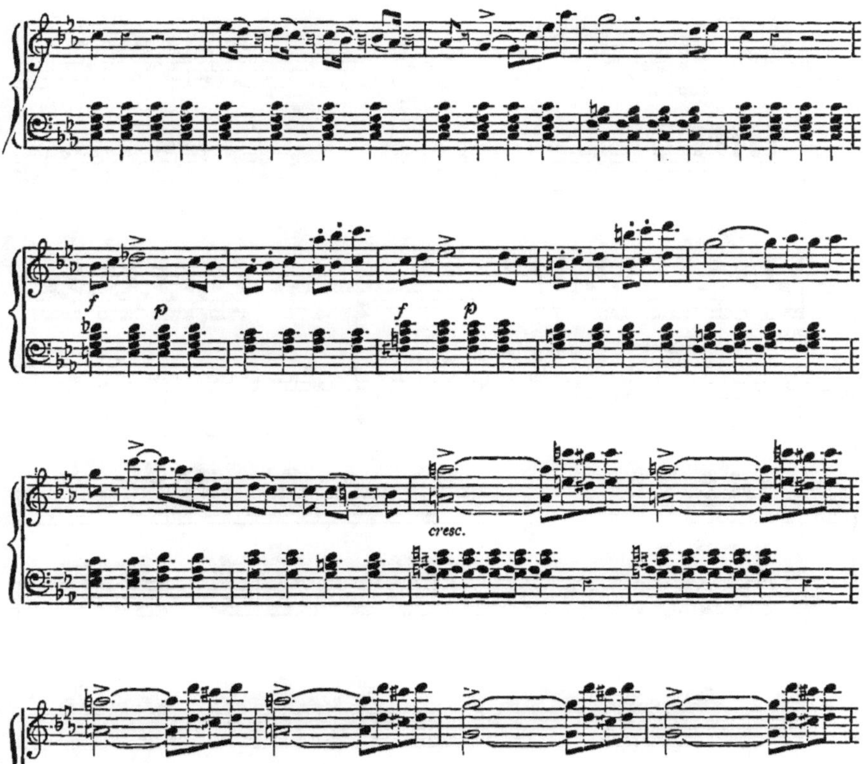
f
p
f
p
cresc.
p
cresc. sempre

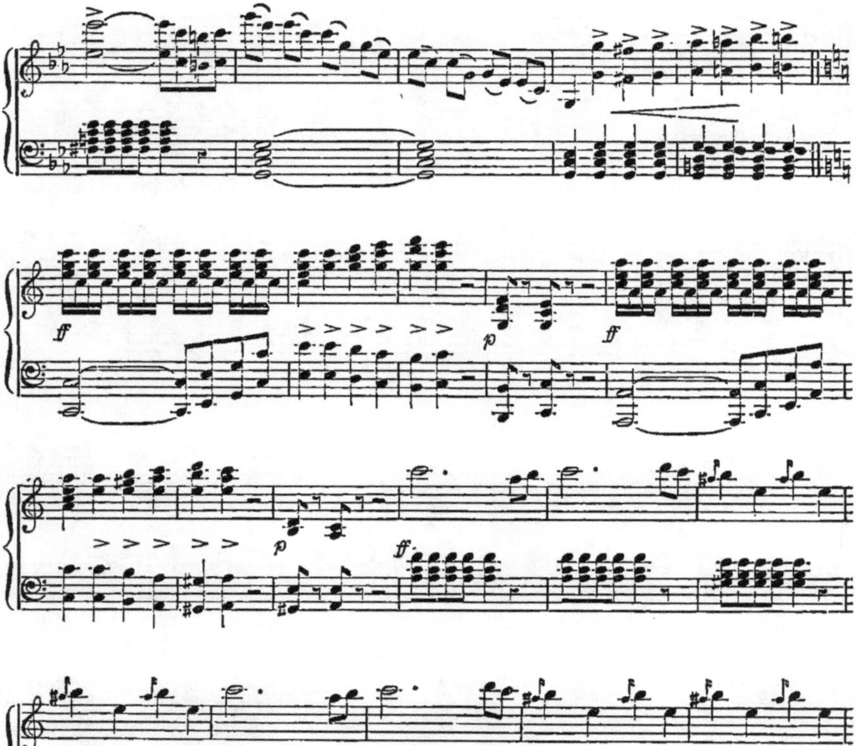
ff
p
ff
p
ff
pp
f

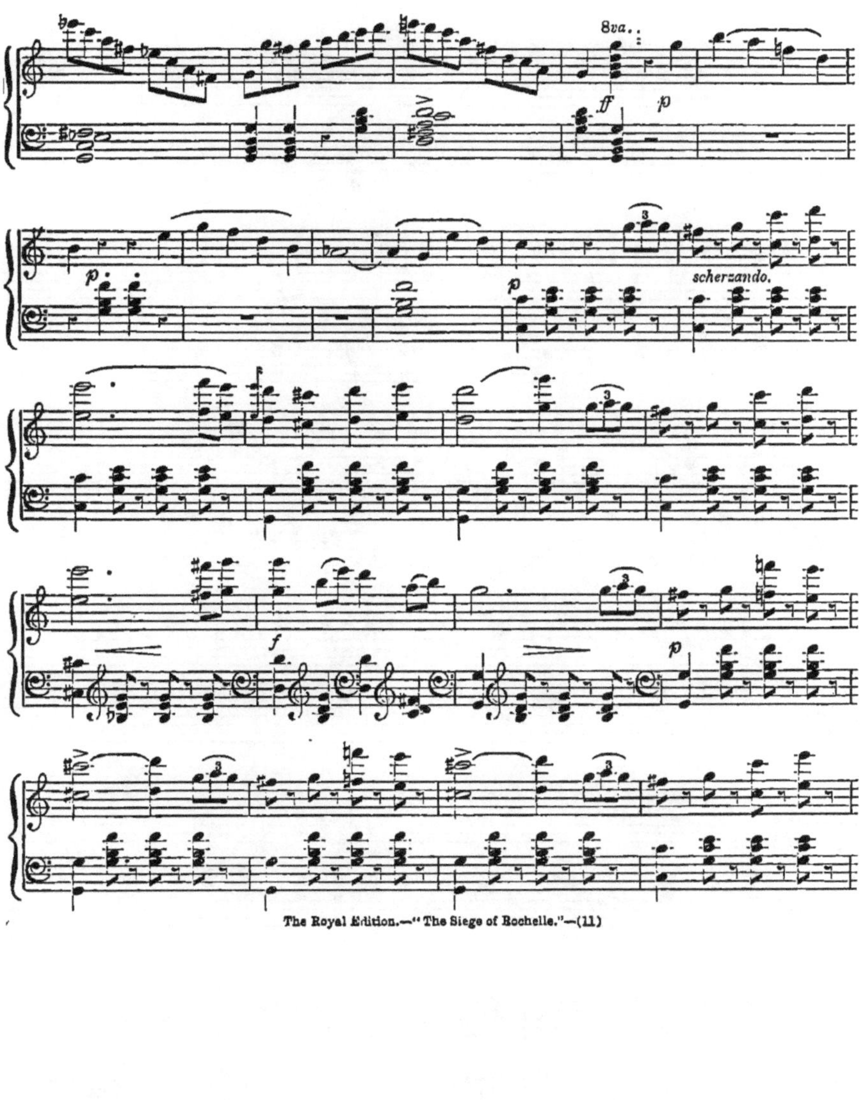
8va.
ff
p
scherzando.
f
3

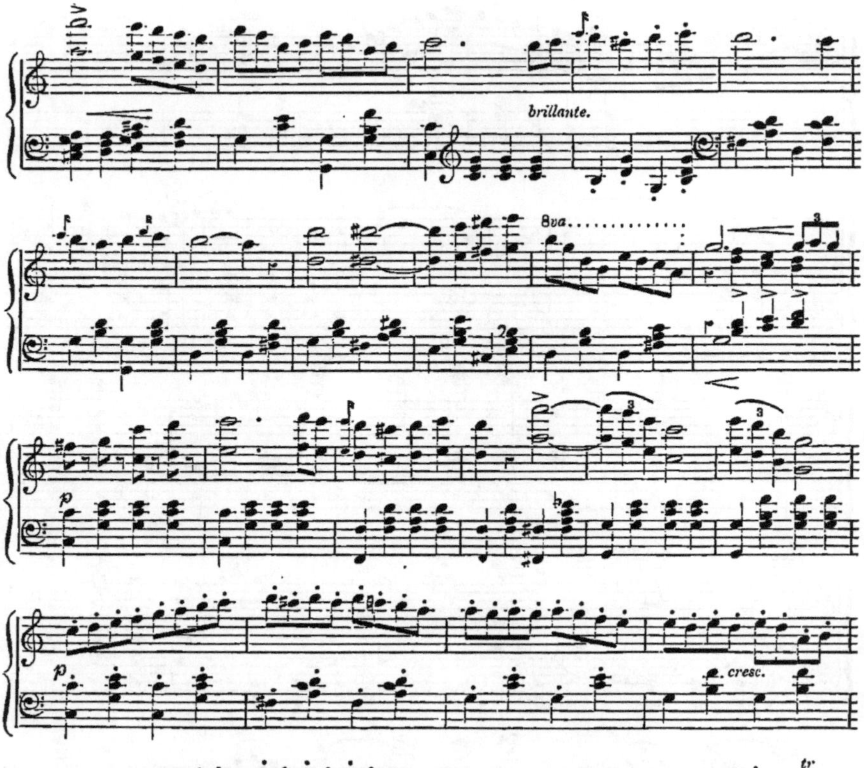
brillante.
8va
p
p
cresc.
tr
ff
tr
p

*stringendo poco a poco.*

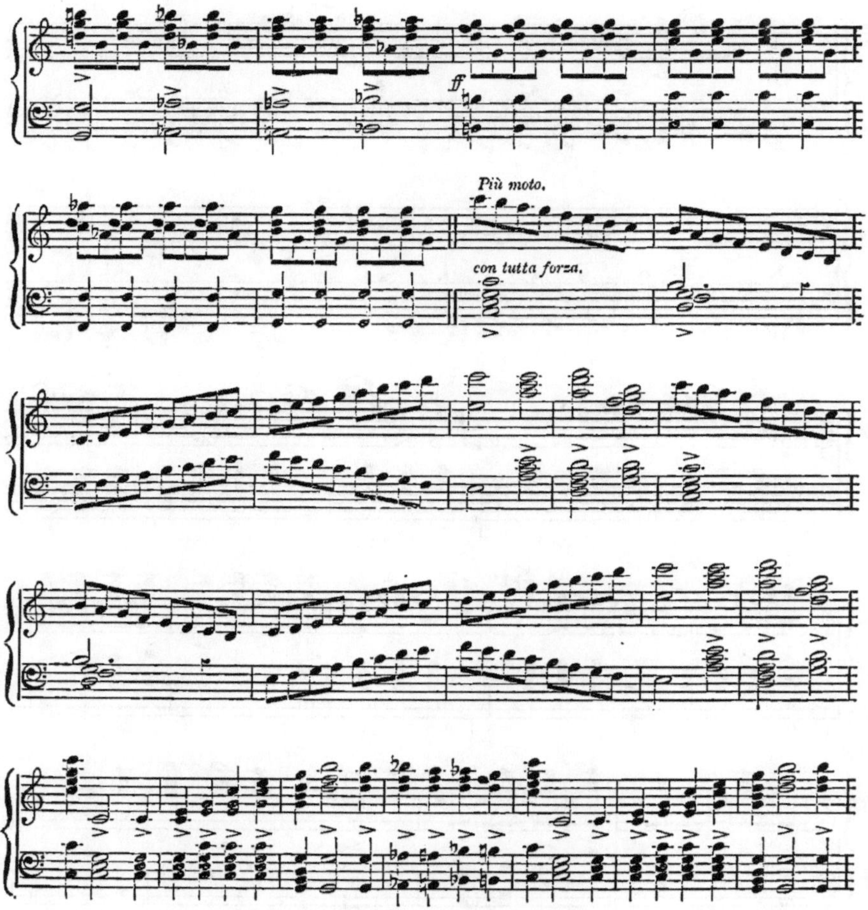
ff
Più moto.
con tutta forza.

# ACT I.

## No. 1. INTRODUCTION AND CHORUS.

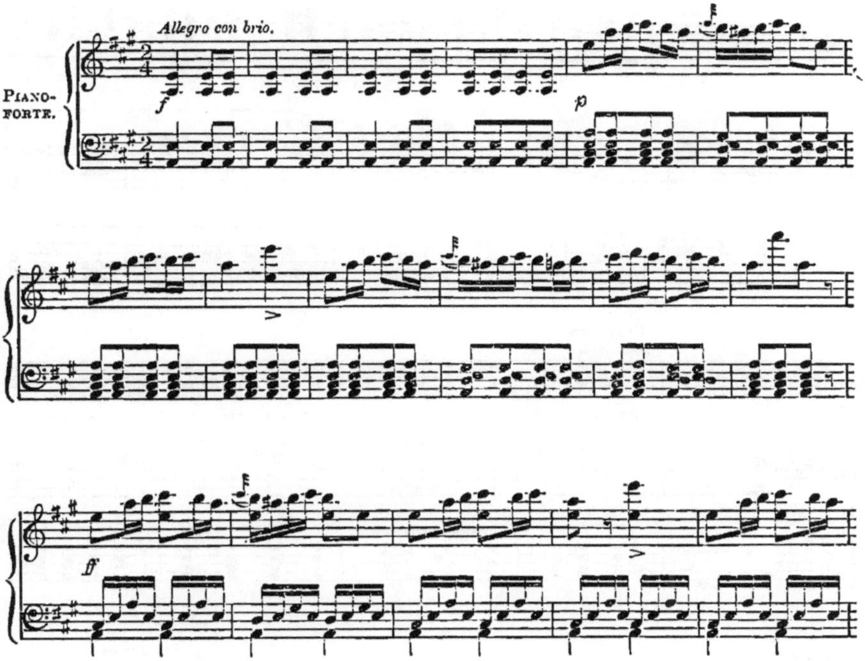

SOLDIERS.

Soli Alti.

Drink, drink to vic - to - ry, re - nown in mar - tial sto - ry;

Drink, drink to vic - to - ry, re - nown in mar - tial sto - ry.

Soli Tenori.

Drink, drink to vic - to - ry, re - nown in mar - tial sto - ry, Drink! drink to vic - to - ry, re -

Alti e Tenori.
-nown in mar-tial sto-ry. To fight, to con-quer, or to sleep, our bed the
Bassi.
To fight, to con-quer, or to sleep, our bed the
ff
field of glo-ry; drink! drink! vic-to-ry! or ours the bed of glo-ry;
field of glo-ry; drink! drink! vic-to-ry! or ours the bed of glo-ry;
drink! drink! vic-to-ry! vic-to-ry! drink! drink!
drink! drink! vic-to-ry! vic-to-ry! drink! drink!
ff
vic-to-ry! vic-to-ry! vic-to-ry!
vic-to-ry! vic-to-ry! vic-to-ry!
p

PEASANTS.
Soprani.

Hark, hark, what bra - ve - ry, all lis - ten to their sto - ry, they

Alti e Tenori.

Hark, hark, what bra - ve - ry, all lis - ten to their sto - ry, they

Bassi.

Hark, hark, what bra - ve - ry, all lis - ten to their sto - ry, they

pp

speak of death as 'twere of sleep, and on - ly dream of glo - ry;

speak of death as 'twere of sleep, and on - ly dream of glo - ry;

speak of death as 'twere of sleep, and on - ly dream of glo - ry;

hark! hark! what bra - ve - ry, all lis - ten to their sto - ry; they

hark! hark! what bra - ve - ry, all lis - ten to their sto - ry; they

hark! hark! what bra - ve - ry, all lis - ten to their sto - ry; they

as 'twere of sleep, and on - ly dream of glo - ry;

as 'twere of sleep, and on - ly dream of glo - ry;

as 'twere of sleep, and on - ly dream of glo - ry;

ric - to - ry, re - nown in mar - tial sto - ry; to fight, to con-quer,

ric - to - ry, re - nown in mar - tial sto - ry; to fight, to con-quer,

bra - ve - ry, all lis - ten to their sto - ry; they speak of death as

bra - ve - ry, all lis - ten to their sto - ry: they speak of death as

bra - ve - ry, all lis - ten to their sto - ry; they speak of death as

or to sleep, our bed the field of glo - ry; drink, drink to
or to sleep, our bed the field of glo - ry; drink, drink to
'twere of sleep, and on - ly dream of glo - ry; hark! hark what
'twere of sleep, and on - ly dream of glo - ry; hark! hark what
'twere of sleep, and on - ly dream of glo - ry; hark! hark what
vic - to - ry, re - nown in mar - tial sto - ry; to fight, to con - quer,
vic - to - ry, re - nown in mar - tial sto - ry; to fight, to con - quer,
bra - ve - ry, all lis - ten to their sto - ry; they speak of death as
bra - ve - ry, all lis - ten to their sto - ry; they speak of death as
bra - ve - ry, all lis - ten to their sto - ry: they speak of death as

or we sleep, our bed the field of glo - ry; drink! drink! vic-to-ry! vic-to-

or we sleep, our bed the field of glo - ry; drink! drink! vic-to-ry! vic-to-

'twere of sleep, and on-ly dream of glo-ry; drink! drink! vic-to-ry! vic-to-

'twere of sleep, and on-ly dream of glo-ry; drink! drink! vic-to-ry! vic-to-

'twere of sleep, and on-ly dream of glo-ry; drink! drink! vic-to-ry! vic-to-

- ry! drink! drink! vic-to-ry! vic-to-ry!

- ry! drink! drink! vic-to-ry! vic-to-ry!

- ry! drink! drink! vic-to-ry! vic-to-ry! but not the bed of

- ry! drink! drink! vic-to-ry! vic-to-ry! but not the bed of

- ry! drink! drink! vic-to-ry! vic-to-ry! but not the bed of

drink! drink!
drink! drink!
glo - - ry, but not the bed of glo - - ry;
glo - - ry, but not the bed of glo - - ry;
glo - - ry, but not the bed of glo - - ry;
tr
tr
tr
tr
p

vic - to - ry, or ours the bed of glo - ry!
vic - to - ry, or ours the bed of glo - ry!
drink! drink! vic - to - ry, but
drink! drink! vic - to - ry, but

not the bed of glo-ry!

not the bed of glo-ry!

Drink! drink to vic-to-ry, re-nown in mar-tial sto-ry;

Drink! drink to vic-to-ry, re-nown in mar-tial sto-ry;

Hark! hark! bra - - ve - - -

Hark! hark! hark! hark! what bra - - ve-ry,

Hark! hark! hark! hark! what bra - - ve-ry,

drink! drink! vic - to - ry, or ours the bed of glo - - ry,

drink! drink! vic - to - ry, or ours the bed of glo - - ry,

- ry, hark! hark what bra - ve - ry,

hark! hark! hark! hark! hark what bra - ve - ry, what bra - ve -

hark! hark! hark! hark! hark what bra - ve - ry,

drink to vic - to - - ry, or ours the

drink to vic - to - ry, drink to vic - to - ry, or

drink to vic - - to - - -

- ry, come drink, come drink, but

drink to vic - to - ry, drink to vic - to - ry, but

bed, the bed of glo - - ry; ours
ours the bed of glo - - ry; ours
- ry, to vic - to - ry, but not
not the bed of glo - - ry, not
not the bed of glo - - ry, not
8va
the bed of glo - - ry, come drink to
the bed of glo - - ry, drink to
the bed of glo - - ry, drink
the bed of glo - - ry; what bra - ve - ry,
the bed of glo - - ry; drink to
8va

vic - to - ry, or ours the bed, the bed of

vic - to - ry, drink to vic - to - ry, or ours the bed of

to vic - to - ry, not bed of

come drink, come drink, bu not the bed of

vic - to - ry, drink to vic - to - ry, but not the bed of

8va..............................

glo - ry, ours the bed of

glo - ry, ours the bed of

glo - ry, not the bed of

glo - ry, not the bed of

glo - ry, not the bed of

8va..............................

glo - - ry, drink, drink to vic - to - ry, vic - to - ry, vic - to -
glo - - ry, drink, drink to vic - to - ry, vic - to - ry, vic - to -
glo - - ry, drink, drink to vic - to - ry, vic - to - ry, vic - to -
glo - - ry, drink, drink to vic - to - ry, vic - to - ry, vic - to -
glo - - ry, drink, drink to vic - to - ry, vic - to - ry, vic - to -
8va
- ry, drink to vic - -
- ry, drink to vic - -
- ry, drink to vic - -
- ry, drink to vic - -
- ry, drink to vic - -

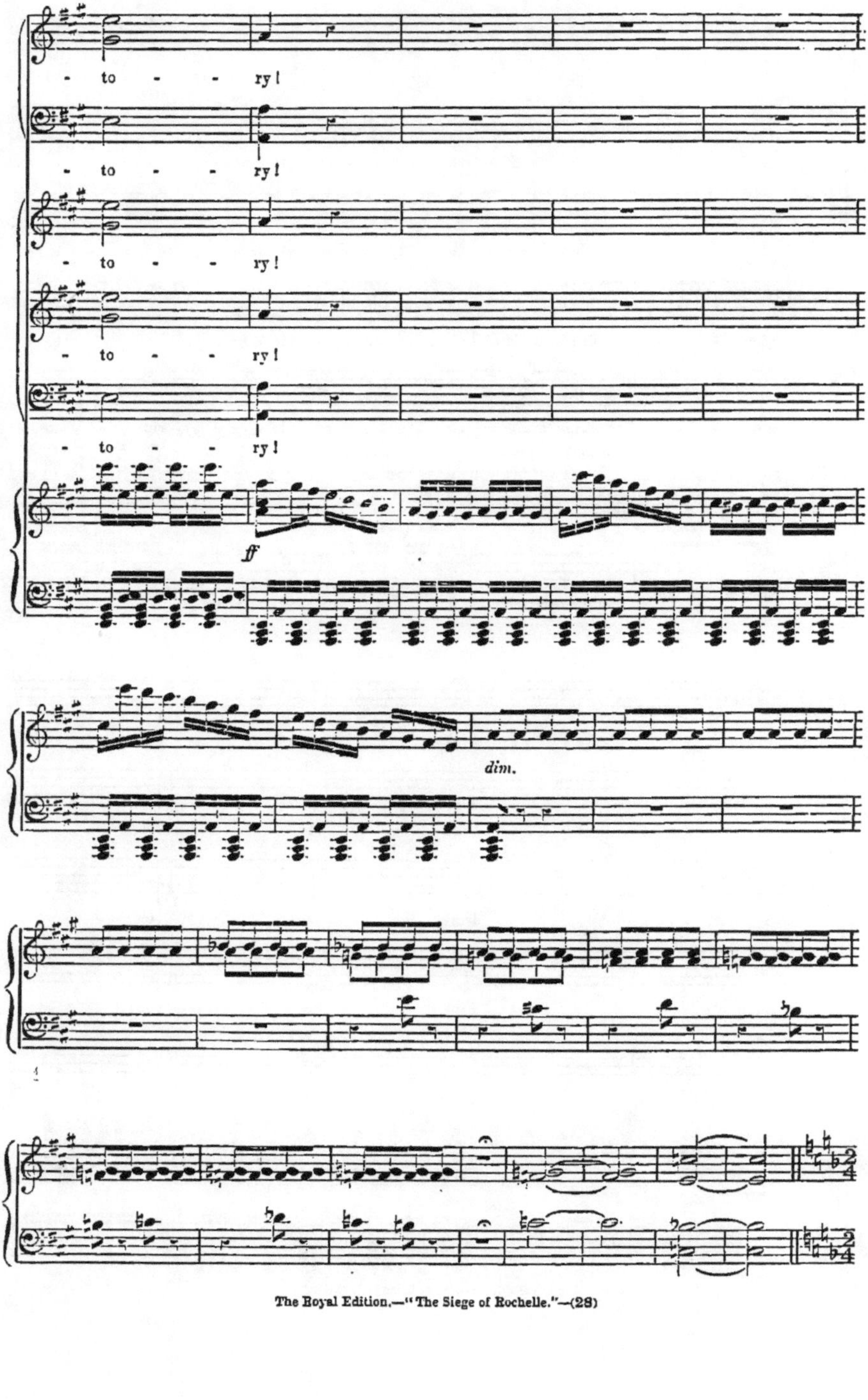
- to - - ry!
- to - - ry!
- to - - ry!
- to - - ry!
- to - - ry!
ff
dim.

No. 1A.                    CAVATINA

*Larghetto.*   MARCELLA.

When, when will he re - turn?

love still pro - longs hope's sto - - ry; too long de - lay'd, our

home he'll find a field of death or glo - - ry.

Love, love haste to me, my

on - ly pride, my glo - ry,

haste, haste, haste my dear Mi - chel,................ my on - ly

love, my on - ly love, my glo - ry,

my on - ly pride, my glo - - - - - ry.

## No. 1B.

Allegro vivace.
tromba.
ff
p
Corporal Schwartz.
Quick march! re-
-lieve the guard, let ev'-ry man at his sta-tion be, and ere an-
-o-ther, an-o-ther watch we see, be death or glo-ry our re-
-ward; and ere an-o-ther, an-o-ther watch we see, be death or
f

glo - ry    our re - ward.    Quick march !
SOLDIERS.
Alti, Tenori, Bassi.

Quick, quick march !    re - lieve the

quick march ! let  ev' - ry  man  at his  sta - tion be,  and

guard,    let  ev' - ry  man  at his  sta  - tion be,  and

ere  an - o - ther watch,    an - o - ther watch we    see,    be  death  or
SOLDIERS.

ere  an - o - ther watch,    an - o - ther watch we    see,    be  death  or
PEASANTS. Soprani e Contralti.

Tenori.                What bra - ve - ry !         what bra - ve - ry !

Bassi.                 What bra - ve - ry !         what bra - ve - ry !

                       What bra - ve - ry !         what bra - ve - ry !

glo - ry our re - ward!

glo - ry our re - ward! Quick, quick march! quick march!

what bra - ve - ry!

what bra - ve - ry!

what bra - ve - ry!

re - lieve the guard, re - lieve the guard, re -

Re - lieve the guard, re -

Re - lieve the guard, re -

Re - lieve the guard, re -

- lieve the guard!

- lieve the guard!

- lieve the guard!

- lieve the guard!

*ff*

MARCELLA.

Heav'n shield the sol - dier's breast, his fate renown'd in

PEASANTS.

*pp staccato sempre.*

Hea - ven shield the sol - dier's breast, his fate re -

Hea - ven shield the sol - dier's breast, his fate re -

*pp*

*p*

*p*

sto - ry to tri-umph proud- ly, or to rest where o'er him beams with glo - ry;

- nown'd in sto - ry, yes, to tri - umph proud - ly,

- nown'd in sto - ry, yes, to tri - umph proud - ly,

Heav'n shield the sol- dier's breast, his fate renown'd in sto - ry to tri-umph proudly,

or to rest where o'er him beams with glo - ry,

or to rest where o'er him beams with glo - ry,

or to rest where o'er him beams with glo - ry! Heav'n shield the sol-dier's breast, his

Hark, hark what bra - ve - ry! oh,

o'er him beams with glo - ry! Hark, hark what bra - ve - ry! oh,

o'er him beams with glo - ry! Hark, hark what bra - ve - ry! oh,

fate renown'd in sto - ry to tri-umph proud-ly, or to rest where o'er him beams with

lis - ten to their sto - ry, they fight, they con - quer or they sleep, dead in the lap of

lis - ten to their sto - ry, they fight, they con - quer, or they sleep, dead in the lap of

lis - ten to their sto - ry, they fight, they con - quer, or they sleep, dead in the lap of glo - ry; Heav'n shield the sol- dier's breast, his fate renown'd in sto - ry to

glo - ry; hark, hark, what bra - ve - ry, oh, lis-ten to their sto - ry; they

glo - ry; hark, hark, what bra - ve - ry, oh, lis-ten to their sto - ry; they

glo - ry; hark, hark, what bra - ve - ry, oh, lis-ten to their sto - ry; they

tri-umph proud-ly, or to rest, where o'er him beams with glo-ry; Hea- ven shield...........

Come, drink to

SOLDIERS.

Come, drink to

fight, they con-quer, or they sleep, dead in the lap of glo - ry; drink

fight, they con-quer, or they sleep, dead in the lap of glo - ry; come and drink,

fight, they con-quer, or they sleep, dead in the lap of glo - ry; drink to

f

vic - to - ry, or ours the bed, the bed of

vic - to - ry, drink to vic - to - ry, or ours the bed of

to vic - to - ry, to vic - to -

come drink, come drink, but not the bed of

vic - to - ry, drink to vic - to - ry, but not the bed of

the sol - dier's, sol - dier's

glo - ry, ours the bed of

- ry, but not the bed of

glo - ry, not the bed of

glo - ry, not the bed of

breast, Hea-ven, Hea-ven shield......................
glo - - ry, come drink to vic - to - ry, or

glo - - ry, driuk to vic - to - ry, drink to

glo - - ry, drink to vic - -

glo - - ry, what bra - ve - ry! come, drink, drink, drink,

glo - - ry, drink to vic - to - ry, drink to

ours the bed, the bed of glo - - ry, the

vic - to - ry, or ours the bed of glo - - ry,

- to - - ry, to vic - to - ry, but

but not the bed of glo - - ry,

vic - to - ry, but not the bed of glo - - ry,

sol - dier's breast, the sol - dier's breast, Heav'n shield the

ours the bed of glo - - ry, drink, drink to

not the bed of glo - - ry, drink, drink to

not the bed of glo - - ry, drink, drink to

not the bed of glo - - ry, drink, drink to

8va.............................................................

sol - dier's breast, Heav'n shield the sol - dier's breast,

vic - to - ry, drink, drink to vic - to - ry,

vic - to - ry, drink, drink to vic - to - ry,

vic - to - ry, drink, drink to vic - to - ry,

vic - to - ry, drink, drink to vic - to - ry,

8va.....

shield    the    sol - - dier's    breast.

drink    to    vic - - to - - ry.

drink    to    vic - - to - - ry.

drink    to    vic - - to - - ry.

drink    to    vic - - to - - ry.

# SONG AND CHORUS.

*Allegro moderato.*

Trav'llers all of ev-'ry sta - tion, trav'l-lers all of ev-'ry sta-tion draw long bows, they draw long bows of ev'ry na - tion; no-thing but ex - ag - ge - ra - tion, no - thing but ex - ag - ge - ra - tion of the climes where they have been, where they have been.    Neigh-bours, since you thus be - seech    me, I'll my lit - tle sto - ry

teach    ye, may such dan-gers nev - er    reach    ye    as have caus'd me fear-ful

strife;    neigh-bours, since you thus be - seech me,    I'll  my  lit - tle sto - ry

teach ye, may such dan - gers nev - er reach ye    as have caus'd me fear - ful

strife, may such dan - gers nev - er reach ye    as have caus'd me fear - ful strife, may such dan - gers nev - er reach ye as have caus'd me fear - ful

strife, as have caus'd me fear-ful strife, may such dan-gers ne - ver reach ye as have caus'd me fear-ful

strife, may such dan - gers nev - er reach ye as have caus'd me fear - ful

strife, may such dan - gers nev - er reach ye as have caus'd me fear - ful

strife, as have caus'd me fear - ful strife; fif - ty storms I have en - dur'd, yes, to dread - ful ills in-nur'd, iu-nur'd; wounded for - ty times aud curd; three times

drown'd and brought to life, three times drown'd and brought to

*Soprani e Contralti.*

N—o!

*Tenori.*

N—o!

*Bassi.*

N—o!

life, three times drown'd and brought to life, three times drown'd and brought to

o—h! three times

o—h! three times

o—h! three times drown'd and brought to

life, three times drown'd and brought to life; monsters hor - rid, past all

drown'd and brought to life!

drown'd and brought to life!

life, three times drown'd and brought to life!

dream - ing, eyes like burn - ing com - ets beam - ing

full up - on me have been gleam - ing, e - ven now my cou - rage

fails, ser - pents I have seen in floods, too, o - thers

Some with bells up - on their

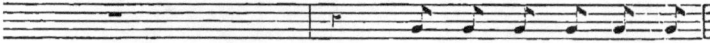

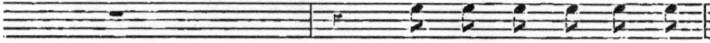

Some with bells up - on their

Some with bells up - on their

ser - pents I have seen in floods, too, o - thers met in drea - ry

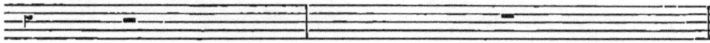

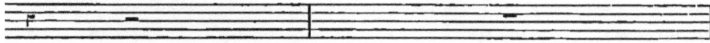

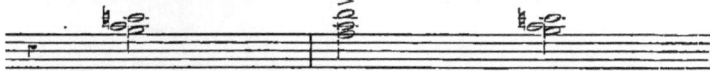

woods, too, some in scales, and some in hoods, too, some with bells up - on their

tails;                          in - to Etna's cra - ter  jum-bled, in - to Et-na's cra-ter

*pp*
Some with bells up-on their  tails!

*pp*
Some with bells up-on their  tails!

*pp*
Some with bells up-on their  tails!

*pp*

jum-bled ere in flames to ash-es  crum - bled;                to Niag-ra's  source I

O—h!

O—h!

O—h!

tum-bled, to Niag-'ra's source I tum-bled, like a fea-ther float-ed forth, to Niag'ra's source I

*cresc.* *dim.*

tum-bled, like a fea-ther float-ed forth

He like a fea-ther float-ed

He like a fea-ther float-ed

He like a fea-ther float-ed

*p*

France and Rus-sia next in - vi-ted, France and Rus-sia next in -

forth!

forth!

forth!

-vi-ted, there the la-dies I de-light-ed, but their gold and beau-ty

slight-ed, but their gold and beau-ty slight-ed, con-scious of Mar-cel-la's

worth, but their gold and beau-ty slight-ed, con-scious of Mar-cel-la's

worth; ta-ken by a cru-el cor-sair, ta-ken by a cru-el

Bra-vo, bra-vo, good Mi-chel!

Bra-vo, bra-vo, good Mi-chel

Bra-vo, bra-vo, good Mi-chel!

cor-sair, horrid whiskers coarse as horse - hair, he'd have made of me a

corse there, he'd have made of me a corse there, but I plung'd in - to the

deep, great es - cape it was, be - lieve me,

O—h!...................

O—h!...............

O—h!................

fish did on its back re-cieve me, a fly - ing fish which soon did leave me on an is-land fast a-sleep, a fly-ing fish which soon did

leave me on an is-land fast a - sleep, on an is - land fast a -

*Soprani e Contralti.*

Fast a - -

- sleep, a fly - ing fish which soon did leave me on an is - land fast a -

- sleep!

- sleep, on an is - land fast a - sleep; there this

fast a - - sleep!

hour I had been stay-ing, but a mer-maid near me stray-ing, thus the

hur-dy-gur-dy play-ing, chang'd it, chang'd it in-to a boat, a boat for

me; ma-gic then en-chant-ing bound me, scarce I saw the waves a-

-round me ere in Lon-don Docks I found me, then St. Paul's just strik-ing

*Allegro vivace.*

three.                                                              Well then, my friends, if you wish to tra - vel, England's the ve - ry best place to see, bet - ter than

Spain, its Dons and Du - en - nas, or France, where folks cry oui, oui, oui; Eng - land's the

gar - den of love - ly wo - men, faith-ful as doves too, the men are all bold, stran - gers grow

8va......................................

rich there, pray where is the won - der? parks, squares, and streets all gra - vel'd with

gold; stran - gers grow rich there, pray where's the won - der? parks, squares, and streets all gra-vel'd with gold; stran-gers grow rich there, pray where's the

won - der? parks, squares, and streets all gra-vel'd with gold; stran-gers grow

rich there, pray where is the won - der? parks, squares, and streets all gra-vel'd with

gold, parks, squares, and streets all gra-vel'd with gold:

All

All

All

in Ger - ma - ny all's ja, ja, in
gra - vel'd with gold! ja, ja, ja,
gra - vel'd with gold! ja, ja, ja,
gra - vel'd with gold! ja, ja, ja,
8va
France 'tis on - ly oui, oui, oui, a fig, too, for
ja, oui, oui, oui, oui,
ja, oui, oui, oui, oui,
ja, oui, oui, oui, oui,
8va
Spain and all its dons, Eng - land's the land to
don, don, don, don,
don, don, don, don,
don, don, don, don,

see, in Ger-ma-ny all's ja, ja, in France 'tis on-ly oui, for

Eng - land's the land to see, Eng -

Eng - land's the land to see, Eng -

Eng - land's the land to see, Eng -

lib - er - ty, beau-ty, and truth Eng-land, England's the land for me, England's the

- land's the land to see,

- land's the land to see,

- land's the land to see,

land, the land to see, Eng-land's the land, the land for me, Eng-land's the

Eng-land's the

Eng-land's the

Eng-land's the

land, the land for me, the land for me! well then, my

land, the land for me, the land for me!

land, the land for me, the land for me!

land, the land for me, the land for me!

friends, if you wish to tra - vel, England's the ve - ry best place to see, bet - ter than

Spain, its Dons and Du - en - nas, or France, where folks cry oui, oui, oui; Eng-land's the

gar - den of love - ly wo - men, faith-ful as doves too, the men are all bold, stran - gers grow rich there, pray where is the won - der? parks, squares, and streets all gra - vel'd with

gold; stran - gers grow rich there, pray where's the won - der? parks, squares, and

streets all gra - vel'd with gold; stran - gers grow rich there, pray where's the

won - der? parks, squares, and streets all gra - vel'd with gold; a fig for

*f*

*p*

Spain, for Ger - ma - ny, Rus - sia, and France, where the peo - ple cry oui, oui, oui,

oui, a fig for Spain, for Ger-ma-ny, Rus-sia, and France, where the peo-ple cry oui, oui, oui,

oui, oui, oui, oui, oui, oui, oui, oui, oui, oui, oui, oui, oui, a fig for Spain, a fig for

Oui, oui, oui, oui, ha! ha! ha!

Oui, oui, oui, oui, ha! ha! ha!

Oui, oui, oui, oui, ha! ha! ha!

France with their oui, oui, oui, oui, oui, oui, oui, oui, oui, oui, a fig for Spain, a fig for

ha!　　oui, oui, oui, oui, ha! ha! ha!

ha!　　oui, oui, oui, oui, ha! ha! ha!

ha!　　oui, oui, oui, oui, ha! ha! ha!

France, Eng-land's the land, the land for me, England's the land, the land for

ha! Eng-land's the land for

ha! Eng-land's the land for

ha! Eng-land's the land for

me, the land for me, the land for me............

me, the land for me, the land for me............

me, the land for me, the land for me............

me, the land for me, the land for me............

# CHORUS.

Soprani e Contralti.
sotto voce.

Swear - ing death to trai - tor slave, hand we clench, sword we draw; heav'n de -

Tenori.

Swear - ing death to trai - tor slave, hand we clench, sword we draw; heav'n de -

Bassi e MICHEL.

Swear - ing death to trai - tor slave, hand we clench, sword we draw; heav'n de -

- fend the true and brave, Vive le Roi! vive le Roi! heav'n de - fend the true and

- fend the true and brave, Vive le Roi! vive le Roi! heav'n de - fend the true and

- fend the true and brave, Vive le Roi! vive le Roi! heav'n de - fend the true and brave, Vive le Roi! vive le Roi! heav'n de - fend the true and brave, Vive le

brave, Vive le Roi! vive le Roi! heav'n de - fend the true and brave, Vive le

brave, Vive le Roi! vive le Roi! heav'n de - fend the true and brave, Vive le

Roi! vive le Roi! Swear-ing death to trai - tor slave, hand we clench, sword we

Roi! vive le Roi! Swear-ing death to trai - tor slave, hand we clench, sword we

Roi! vive le Roi! Swear-ing death to trai - tor slave, hand we clench, sword we

draw; heav'n de - fend the true and brave, Vive le Roi! vive le Roi!

draw; heav'n de - fend the true and brave, Vive le Roi! vive le Roi!

draw; heav'n de - fend the true and brave, Vive le Roi! vive le Roi!

*sotto voce.*

Hearts that pa - triot thoughts in - spire, re - bel threat ne'er shall awe! thus, till

Hearts that pa - triot thoughts in - spire, re - bel threat ne'er shall awe! thus, till

Hearts that pa - triot thoughts in - spire, re - bel threat ne'er shall awe! thus, till

*p*

life's last throb ex - pire, Vive le Roi! vive le Roi! yes, till life's last throb ex -

life's last throb ex - pire, Vive le Roi! vive le Roi! yes, till life's last throb ex -

life's last throb ex - pire, Vive le Roi! vive le Roi! yes, till life's last throb ex -

- pire, Vive le Roi! vive le Roi! yes, till life's last throb ex - pire, Vive le

- pire, Vive le Roi! vive le Roi! yes, till life's last throb ex - pire, Vive le

- pire, Vive le Roi! vive le Roi! yes, till life's last throb ex - pire, Vive le

Roi! vive le Roi! Hearts that pa - triot thoughts in - spire, re - bel threat ne'er shall

Roi! vive le Roi! Hearts that pa - triot thoughts in - spire, re - bel threat ne'er shall

Roi! vive le Roi! Hearts that pa - triot thoughts in - spire, re - bel threat ne'er shall

awe! thus, till life's last throb ex - pire, Vive le Roi! vive le Roi!

awe! thus, till life's last throb ex - pire, Vive le Roi! vive le Roi!

awe! thus, till life's last throb ex - pire, Vive le Roi! vive le Roi!

# ROMANCE.

*'Mid the scenes of ear-ly youth, mem-'ry still delights to stray; scenes re-plete with love and truth, fa-ded now a-way! where those bow'rs of myr-tle wreath in that maze, that maze of stream.... and tree,.............. beats there still a heart to breathe one sad*

sigh for me, one sad sigh, one sad sigh for me?

_ad lib. e lento._

one sad sigh, one sad sigh.................... for me?

Spark-ling do those fountains flow as when there I tun'd my lute?.... doth some

o - ther charm him now, is he still as mute? tho' it break be-neath the wrong, still con - tent, con - tent my heart...... would be..............might a

note of her sweet voice wake one sigh for me, wake one sigh, one sad

sigh for me, one sad sigh, one sad sigh.............. for

me.

# RECITATIVE AND CAVATINA.

VALMOUR.

Why seeks my soul in ev-'ry face that on-ly look of her's to trace? sweet poi-son flow'r, thy hon — ied breath but once, but once im-bib'd our love    is death.

In    vain...... my soul her im - age flies,......... no

dream of hope, no dream of hope sub - dues    my    woes,    deep    in this heart love's

ma - gic lies,    deep    as the can - ker in the rose,......... deep as the can - ker, as the can - ker in the rose; my halls for her, for her are

de - so - late, tears........ yield a - lone re -

- lief, they sad - - ly soothe my deep de -

- spair,.... my on - ly joy is grief, my on - ly joy,.... my on - ly joy is

grief.................... In vain..... my soul her im - age flies,......... no dream of hope, no dream of hope sub-dues my woes, deep in this heart love's ma - gic

lies,............ deep as the can-ker, as the can-ker in the rose,........... deep as the

can - ker, as the can - ker in the rose, as the can - ker in........ the

rose.

*Allegro moderato.*

Hope, once more this bo - som fill, mine the

wreath of mar - tial pride, va - lour ev - 'ry nerve shall

thrill, hon - our, hon - our be my bride; where some

mourn - ful cy - press weeps, on the cold earth's tran - quil

breast,.................... where the brave heart no - bly

sleeps, there I'll seek, I'll seek my rest; where the

brave heart no - bly sleeps,...... there I'll seek, I'll seek my

rest; where the brave heart no - - bly sleeps, there I'll

cresc.

seek, there I'll seek my..... rest;

where the brave heart no - bly sleeps,

cresc.

there I'll seek, I'll seek my

rest; where the brave heart no - bly sleeps, there I'll

seek, I'll seek my rest; there I'll seek my

rest.

Hope, once more this bo - som fill, mine the

wreath of mar - tial pride, va - lour ev - 'ry nerve shall

thrill, hon - our, hon - our be my bride; where some

mourn - ful cy - press weeps, on the cold earth's tran - quil

breast,...................... where the brave heart no - bly sleeps,         there I'll   seek, I'll seek     my     rest;    where    the

brave    heart no  -  bly sleeps,...... there    I'll  seek,   I'll seek    my

rest;    where    the  brave      heart no  -  -  bly  sleeps, there  I'll

cresc.

seek,   there  I'll  seek  my    rest,    there   I'll seek      my rest, there I'll seek my rest, there......  .............

*fp*    *fp*    *fp*    *fp*    *ff*

......  I'll seek,........ I'll seek my

rest.

# DUET.

*Allegretto.*

PIANO-FORTE.

MICHEL.

Well, if I must speak my mind 'twere strange, I say, with-out dis-guise, did not these fea-tures

sometimes find fa-vour in sweet la-dies' eyes: I have tra-vell'd, I am fin-ish'd;

if soft looks kind thought pro-claim, beau-ties sigh-ing, for me dy-ing, can I help it, who's to blame? can I help it, can I help it, who's to blame?

can I help it, can I help it, who's to blame?

MARCELLA.

Well, sir, ful-ly as sin-cere I have been told, no mat-ter when, these eyes of mine some-

-times ap - pear sunshine to the gen-tle-men; with this face, sir, and this form, sir,

if soft locks fond hopes proclaim, young men sigh-ing, for one dy - ing, hus-band roaming, who's to blame? hus - band roam - ing, hus - band roam - ing, who's to blame?

hus - band roam - ing, hus - band roam - ing, who's to blame?

MICHEL.

In my ab-sence

MARCELLA.

who has dar'd to breathe to you his wi - ly sighs? Frown not, dar - ling,

lest those fea - tures loose their charms in la - dies' eyes. Sometimes

Say, where was it?

walk-ing,            sometimes talk-ing,

say, how came it?        where on earth could this have

sometimes danc-ing on the green.

been?     In my ab-sence, me un-do-ing, quick re-veal each

vil-lain's name; oh! tor-ment-ing! bil-ling, coo-ing, I'll soon teach them who's to

blame; nev-er more my home I'll leave if to

me you'll prove but true. Nev - er more will I de -

- ceive if you think those eyes will do. I tor -

MICHEL.

I was jen-lous,

- ment - ing, thus for - give - ness we pro - claim, love con - fi - ding, no more

thus for - give - ness we pro - claim, love con - fi - ding, no more

*colla parte.*

*rall.*

chi - ding, we a - like are both to blame, we a - like are both to blame.

chi - ding, we a - like are both to blame, we a - like are both to blame.

MARCELLA.
Thus to - ge - ther, side by side, love, like two ring - doves,
Tempo di Waltz. p
we will stray, we will stray; yes, u - nit - ed.... we through life
8va
or
MICHEL.
will sing and dance, and laugh and play. Thus to - ge - ther
8va...
side by side...... love, like two ring-doves we will stray,.......

..... yes, u - nit - ed we thro' life will sing and dance, and
laugh and play, yes, u - nit - ed we..... thro' life will
sing, will sing, and laugh, and play,........... still to - ge - ther;
some-times walk-ing, laugh-ing, talk-ing,
al - ways mer - ry,

where our friends are we'll be seen, be seen, some-times danc - ing

where our friends are we'll be seen, be seen, some-times danc - ing

on the green, la, la, la, la, la, la, la, la, la, la, la, la, la, la, la, la,

on the green, la, la, la, la, la, la, la, la, la,

la, la, la, la, la, la, la, la, la, la, la, la, la, la, la, la, la, la, la, la, la, la, la, la,

la, la, la, la, la, la, la, la, la, la, la, la, la, la, la,

la, la, la, la, la, la, la, la, la, thus to - ge - ther.... side by...... side,

la, la, la, la, la, la, la, la, la, thus to - ge - ther.... side by...... side, love, like two ring-doves we will stray, we will stray, yes, u - nit - ed.....

love, like two ring-doves we will stray, we will stray, yes, u - nit - ed.....

or

we through life will sing and dance, and laugh and play,

we through life will sing and dance, and laugh and play,

yes, we'll sing, we'll laugh and play, yes, we'll dance and

yes, we'll sing, we'll laugh and play, yes, we'll dance and

sing    and  play,    we'll  laugh  and    play,    we'll  laugh  and

sing    and  play,    we'll  laugh  and    play,    we'll  laugh  and

play,         we'll  laugh  and   play.

play,         we'll  laugh  and   play.

# QUARTET.

I am a-lone a-gain! a-lone! a-lone! my heart's de—spair, in—dulge thy care a—lone in this wide world of sor - row,     in this wild     world     of     sor  -  row!

CLARA.

Oh! Vir - gin, pi - ty me!

oh hear,       oh     hear,     my     bo - - som's

fears     dis - solve           in     tears,     and

teach     me hope from thee     to     bor - row,     and teach me hope to bor -

- row!

*Andante.* VALMOUR.

*rall.*

cresc.

*pp*

Sweet blos - som of pa - ren - tal

joy,     fro - zen too  soon thy in  -  fant  breath, thy in - fant breath;

these spark-ling eyes, my murder'd  boy,.......... they bless thy  fa - ther e'en     in

CLARA.

death!          Oh,  Vir - gin, his each earth-ly  joy,      for  him I

*pp*

pray with fer - vent breath, with fer - vent breath! these gush ing tears with-out al -

- loy,......... for his re - pose could flow till death! VALMOUR. yes, these

These speak-ing eyes, my

gush - ing tears, yes,......... for his re - pose, these

mur - der'd boy, they bless thy fa - ther e'en in death, they

gush - ing tears...... for his re - pose could flow till death, yes, till

bless thy fa - ther, they bless thy fa - ther e'en in death, e'en in death, for his re - pose could flow till death, yes, till death, for...... his re-

death, they..... bless thy fa - ther e'en in death, e'en in death, they.... bless thy

- pose could flow till death, till death, till...... death!

fa - ther, e'en in death, in death, in...... death!

*Allegro.*

*Moderato.* VALMOUR.

No eye.......... ob-serves my

guil - ty love, for oh, I can-not quell its glow, sweet look thus cloth'd in

in - no-cence, oh, Cla - ra, oh, Cla-ra, is it thou! no eye observes my

guil - ty love, for oh, I can-not quell its glow, no, sweet look thus cloth'd in

in - no-cence, oh, Cla - ra, oh, Cla - ra, is it thou!

*pp*

CLARA.

That plain-tive voice so soft and sad, Heav'ns! methinks its tone I know, Heav'ns! me - thinks...... its tone I know;.......... like some....... for-got-ten me - lo-dy which sweet - ly thrills, but thrills with woe,          like     some........ for - got - ten

VALMOUR.

Oh, Cla - ra, is it thou!

me - lo - dy, which sweet - ly thrills with woe.    Yes,     yes,     a - gain it

Cla - ra, is it thou!

speaks of me! Oh, Vir - gin, calm this bo-som's glow, Heav'ns! so near,  great pow'r, my

*Allegro agitato.*    VALMOUR.

rea - son spare! Val - mour, Val - mour, is  it  thou!          What

*f marcato assai.*

piercing cry as-sails mine ear? deep
sobs, a sti-fled groan I hear!
that life-less form, what kin-dred

MARCELLA.

O-
care here al-so wa-kens dark de-spair!
MICHEL.
O-

- lym - pia, what sud - den

Poor life - less

- lym - pia, yes, what sud-den, sud-den care hath

care, what sud - den care

form, hear, Heav'n, my pray'r,

plung'd her thus in dark de - spair? oh, Heav'n, what sud-den, sud-den

hath plung'd her thus in dark de -

and wake her from this dark de -

care hath plung'd her thus in dark de - spair, in dark de -

- spair?      Cla - ra,      that

- spair!      Great pow'r!      Cla - ra, and a - live!

- spair?      Cla - ra,      that

name!

breathe not the sound,      'tis she! how could she thus sur -

name!

Cla - ra,    her name!

- vive?      breathe not the sound,      a

Cla - ra,    her name!

*cresc.*

se - cret 'tis pro - found, let her not
We'll prove sin - cere,
know that I was here, for her re -
We'll prove sin - cere,
we swear! we swear!
- pose to prove sin - cere.
we swear! we swear!

Allegro assai.
Clara.
My rea - - son wakes as from a
dream,.................. a - gain wild thoughts my fan - cy
warm,.................. a trou - bled light steals o'er my
soul,.................. like........ sun - shine through the
storm;.................. a trou - bled light steals o'er my
p
fp
cresc.

soul,.................. like sun - shine thro' the

storm, like........... sun - - - shine,....... like

sun - - - - - - shine through................. the

CLARA.

storm.
MARCELLA.
My rea - son wakes as from a

Her sen - ses wake as from a
VALMOUR.

Her sen - ses wake as from a
MICHEL.

Her rea - son wakes, I must be

Her sen - ses wake as from a

dream, a - gain wild thoughts my fan - cy
dream, life tints once more those fea - tures
gone, nor stay to view the dan-g'rous
dream, life tints once more those fea - tures
warm; a trou - bled light steals o'er my
warm; a trou - bled light beams in her
form; since in this breast can beam no
warm; a trou - bled light beams in her
8va
soul, like............ sun - shine through........ the
eye, like........... sun - shine through......... the
more, the........... sun - shine of............ the
eye, like........... sun - shine through.......... the
8va
fz
fz

sun - shine through....... the

sun - shine through........ the

sun - shine of............ the

sun - shine through....... the

rea - - son wakes as from a dream,.................

rea - - son wakes as from a dream,...............

her rea - son

her rea - son

pp          fp                    fp                    fp

Voice 1: ...... a - gain wild thoughts my fan - cy warm;............

Voice 2: ...... life tints once more those fea - tures warm;............

Voice 3: wakes, I must be gone, I must be gone;............

Voice 4: wakes as from a dream, from a dream:

fp   fp   fp   fp

Voice 1: ...... a trou - bled light steals o'er my soul,............

Voice 2: ...... a trou - bled light beams in her eye,............

Voice 3: since in this

Voice 4: a trou - bled

fp   fp   fp   fp

Voice 1: ...... like sun - shine through the storm;............

Voice 2: ...... like sun - shine through the storm;............

Voice 3: breast can beam no more, can beam no more,............

Voice 4: light beams in her eye, beams in her eye,............

fp

...... a trou - bled light steals o'er my soul,..................
...... a trou - bled light beams in her eye,..................
...... since in this breast can beam,..........
...... a trou-bled light..................................
...... like sun - shine through the storm, like..........
...... like sun - shine through the storm, like..........
...... can beam no more, more, the
...... beams in her eye,...................... like
...... sun - - - shine,.......... like sun - -
.... sun - - - shine,.......... like sun - - -
sun - - - - shine, the sun - - -
sun - - - shine, like sun - - -

shine through.................. the storm; a trou-bled
shine through................. the storm; a trou-bled
shine of.......... the.......... storm; since in this
shine in the storm; a
ff
light.................. steals o'er my soul.................. steals o'er my
light... ................ beams in her eye..................... beams in her
breast.................. can beam no more.................. can beam no
trou-bled, trou-bled light beams in her eye, beams
dim.
soul................ like sun-shine through the storm,............
eye,............... like sun-shine through the storm,...............
dim.
more............ the sun-shine of the storm..............
in her eye, like sun-shine in the storm,.............
dim.

like............ sun - shine through the

like............ sun - shine through the

the............ sun - shine of the

like............ sun - shine through the

*più mosso.*

storm, like sun - shine through the storm,

storm, like sun - shine through the storm,

storm, the sun - shine of the storm,

storm, like sun - shine through the storm,

like sun - - - - - - - shine, like sun - shine
like sun - - - - - - - shine, like sun - shine
the sun - - - - - - - shine................
like sun - - - - - - - shine................
8va.....................................
through.................................... the storm.
through.................................... the storm.
of.................................... the storm.
through.................................... the storm.
8va.....................................
ff Ped.
ff

No. 8                    QUARTET.

Lo! the ear - ly beam of morn - ing

soft - ly chides our longer stay; hark! the ma - tin bells are chim - ing,

Daugh - ter, we must hence a - way, daugh - ter, we must hence a - way;

CLARA.

Fa - ther, I at once at - tend thee, fare-well, friends, for you I'll pray ;

lo ! the ear-ly beam of morn - ing, of morn - ing soft-ly chides our

hark ! the ma - tin bells are chim - ing, fa - ther, we must hence a -

stay ; hark ! the ma - tin bells are chim - - - -

- way, fa - - - ther, we must hence a - way ;

- ing, are chim - ing, daughter, we must hence a -

**CLARA.**

fa - ther, I at once at - tend thee, fare - well, friends, for you I'll

**MARCELLA.**

La - dy, may each blessing wait thee, we for thee will ev - er

**MICHEL.**

La - dy, may each blessing wait thee, we for you will ev - er

**AZINO.**

- way, the ear - ly beam of morn - ing soft - ly chides our long - er

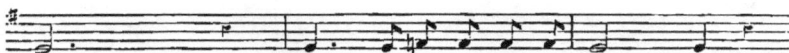

*pp*

pray; hark! the ma - tin bells are chim - ing,

pray; hark! the ma - tin bells are chim - ing,

pray, we for you will ev - er pray; the ma - tin bells are chim - ing,

stay; hark! the ma - tin bells are chim - ing,

fa - ther, we must haste a - way, yes, we must haste a - way;

from all dan-ger haste a - way, from........ all dan-ger haste a - way;

from all dan-ger haste a - way, la - dy, yes, haste a - way;

daugh - ter, we must haste a - way, daugh - ter, hence, hence a - way;

*cresc.*

*p*

*sotto voce.*

fa - ther, I at once at - tend thee, fare - well, friends, for you I'll

la - dy, may each bless - ing wait thee, we for you will ev - er

la - dy, may each bless - ing wait thee, we for you will ev - er

lo! the ear - ly beam of morn - ing soft - ly chides our long-er

*pp*

pray;...... hark! the ma-tin bells are chim - ing, fa - ther, we must hence a -

pray; hark! the ma-tin bells are chim - ing, from all dan-ger haste a -

pray; hark! the ma-tin bells are chim - ing, from all dan-ger haste a -

stay; hark! the ma-tin bells are chim - ing, daugh - ter, we must haste a -

- way, hence a - way,......... hence a - way,........... hence a - way,

- way, haste a - way,........... haste a - way, ........... haste a - way,

- way, haste a - way, haste a - way; ah!

- way, hence a - way, hence a - way, hence a - way,

hence a - way,

hence a - way,

la - dy, may each bless-ing wait thee, we for you will ev - er

hence a - way,

hence a - way, hence a - way,

hence a - way, hence a - way,

pray; hark! the ma-tin bells are chim - ing, from all dan-ger haste a -

hence a - way, hence a - way,

fa - - - ther, we must hence a - way, hence a-

a - way, haste a-

- way, from........ all dan-ger haste a - way, la - dy, haste a - way, haste a-

a - way, hence a-

- way, hence a - way...............................

- way, haste a - way...............................

- way, la - dy, haste a - way, haste a - way...............................

- way, hence a - way...............................

tremolo...............................

# FINALE.

Fa-ther A-zi-no, we have sought you, ho-ly fa-ther, be to us a sa-cred shield; hark! the fierce at-tack com-men-ces,

car - nage fills the bat - tle
ff Clara and Marcella.
Hor - ror! hor - ror!
ff Michel and Azino.
Hor - ror! hor - ror!
ff Soprani e Contralti.
field. Hor - ror! hor - ror!
ff Tenori.
Hor - ror! hor - ror!
ff Bassi.
Hor - ror! hor - ror!
ff
what de - struc - tion, swords are
what de - struc - tion, swords are
what de - struc - tion, swords are
what de - struc - tion, swords are
what de - struc - tion, swords are

clash - ing, guns are flash - ing,

clash - ing, guns are flash - ing,

clash - ing, guns are flash - ing,

clash - ing, guns are flash - ing,

clash - ing, guns are flash - ing,

guard us, migh - ty pow'r, guard us, migh - ty

guard us, migh - ty pow'r, guard us, migh - ty

guard us, migh - ty pow'r, guard us, migh - ty

guard us, migh - ty pow'r, guard us, migh - ty

guard us, migh - ty pow'r, guard us, migh - ty

pow'r ... guard, ... guard

pow'r, ... guard, ... guard

pow'r, ... guard, ... guard

pow'r, ... guard, ... guard

pow'r, ... guard, ... guard

us, ... migh - - - - ty ... pow'r!

us, ... migh - - - - ty ... pow'r!

us, ... migh - - - - ty ... pow'r!

us, ... migh - - - - ty ... pow'r!

us, ... migh - - - - ty ... pow'r!

*fff*

# PRAYER.

GENERAL CHORUS. *(All kneeling.)*
CLARA *and Soprani.*
*sotto voce.*

MARCELLA *and Contralti.*
Oh, Thou, who look'st up - on the bat - tle, and shield - est those Thy love would spare,

*Tenori.*
Oh, Thou, who look'st up - on the bat - tle, and shield - est those Thy love would spare,

*Bassi.*
Oh Thou, who look'st up - on the bat - tle, and shield - est those Thy love would spare,

ex - tend o'er us Thy migh - ty fa - vour, and shel - ter us be - neath Thy care;

ex - tend o'er us Thy migh - ty fa - vour, and shel - ter us be - neath Thy care;

ex - tend o'er us Thy migh - ty fa - vour, and shel - ter us be - neath Thy care;

on our sins now look down in mer-cy, nor for-mer ill dis-pleas'd re-sent, oh,

on our sins now look down in mer-cy, nor for-mer ill dis-pleas'd re-sent, oh,

on our sins now look down in mer-cy, nor for-mer ill dis-pleas'd re-sent, oh,

Thou, who know'st our ev-'ry feel-ing, and grant us lei-sure to re-pent, and grant us

Thou, who know'st our ev-'ry feel-ing, and grant us lei-sure to re-pent,

Thou, who know'st our ev-'ry feel-ing, and grant us lei-sure to re-pent,

lei-sure to re-pent, lei-sure to re-pent, to re-pent.

and grant us lei-sure to re-pent, lei-sure to re-pent, to re-pent.

yes, to re-pent, to re-pent.

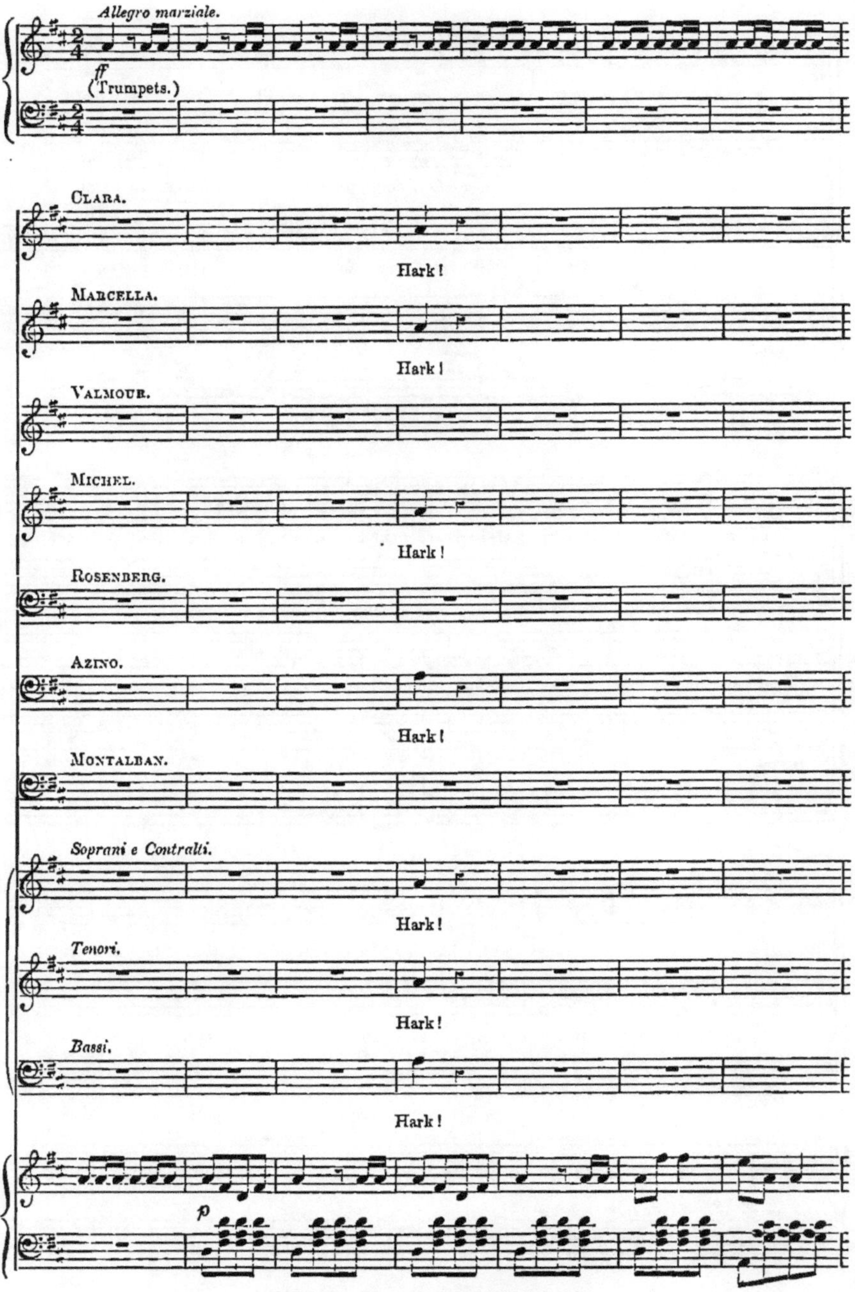
Allegro marziale.
ff
(Trumpets.)
Clara.
Hark!
Marcella.
Hark!
Valmour.
Michel.
Hark!
Rosenberg.
Azino.
Hark!
Montalban.
Soprani e Contralti.
Hark!
Tenori.
Hark!
Bassi.
Hark!
p

hark!   hark! that sound, the strife is o'er, our

hark   hark! that souud, the strife is o'er, our

hark!   hark! that sound, the strife is o'er, our

hark!   hark! that sound, the strife is o'er, our

hark!   hark! that sound, the strife is o'er, our

hark!   hark! that sound, the strife is o'er, our

hark!   hark! that sound, the strife is o'er, our

pray'r is heard, war reigns no more,

pray'r is heard, war reigns no more,

pray'r is heard, war reigns no more,

pray'r is heard, war reigns no more,

our pray'r is

pray'r is heard, war reigns no more,

pray'r is heard, war reigns no more,

pray'r is heard, war reigns no more,

our pray'r is heard, war reigns no more,

our pray'r is heard, war reigns no more,

our pray'r is heard, war reigns no more,

heard, our pray'r is heard, war reigns no more,

our pray'r is heard, war reigns no more,

our pray'r is heard, war reigns no more,

our pray'r is heard, war reigns no more,

our pray'r is    heard, war  reigns  no     more.

our    pray'r is    heard, war  reigns no    more.

our    pray'r is    heard, war reigns no     more.

our  pray'r is    heard,  our  pray'r is    heard, war  reigns no    more.

our    pray'r is    heard, war  reigns  no    more.

our    pray'r is    heard, war reigns no    more.

our    pray'r is    heard, war reigns no    more.

VALMOUR.

Fly, wretch-ed one, the foe re - pell'd, and dri - ven to their walls a - gain, your

*pp*

fa - ther and the count ad - vance to join a re - quiem for the slain!

CLARA.

Oh,

let me hence, oh, hap - less fate, from his ap - proach I fly too late!

ROSENBERG.

That guil - ty

ROSENBERG.

wretch!

know they here her ha - ted

MONTALBAN.

It is the same!

*Allegro.*

*p*

K

name?

Cla - ra Mon-tal - ban, name re-vil'd, as - sas-sin of De Val-mour's

Too wretch-ed daughter, thus re - vil'd, could

That fran - tic air, that an - guish wild, could

Too wretched daugh-ter, could

Cla - ra Mon-tal - ban, as -

Too wretched daugh-ter, could

child! that fiend re - vil'd, as - sas-sin of De Val - mour's

Cla - ra Mon-tal - ban, as -

Cla - ra Mon-tal - ban, as -

Cla - ra Mon-tal - ban, as -

I am not guil - ty, this load of

she de-stroy a help - less child?

she de-stroy a help - less child?

she de-stroy a help - less child?

- sas - sin of De Val - mour's child!

she de-stroy a help - less child?

child!

- sas - sin of De Val - mour's child!

- sas - sin of De Val - mour's child!

- sas - sin of De Val - mour's child!

shame I can - not bear; no, I'll pro - claim the mur - d'rer's name!

Pro - claim, pro - claim the mur - d'rer's name!

Pro - claim, pro - claim the mur - d'rer's name!

Pro - claim, pro - claim the mur - d'rer's name!

Pro - claim, pro - claim the mur - d'rer's name!

Will she pro - claim the mur - d'rer's name?

Will she pro - claim the mur - d'rer's name? Be -

Pro - claim, pro - claim the mur - d'rer's name!

Pro - claim, pro - claim the mur - d'rer's name!

Pro - claim, pro - claim the mur - d'rer's name!

-neath this sa - cred roof beware, a bro - ken oath, a

The murd'rer's name de - clare, de -

The murd'rer's name de - clare, de -

The murd'rer's name de - clare, de -

bro - ken oath he will not spare!

The murd'rer's name de - clare, de -

The murd'rer's name de - clare, de -

The murd'rer's name de - clare, de -

The murd'rer's name de - clare, de -

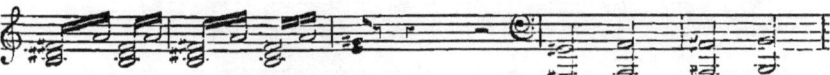

_pp_

The Royal Edition.—"The Siege of Rochelle."—(133)

It is too much, my soul's af - fec-tion;

- clare !

- clare !

- clare !

- clare !

- clare !

begone, and save from death thy soul !

- clare !

- clare !

- clare !

- clare !

cresc.    a poco.

yes, I will speak,    yes, I will speak!

MONTALBAN.

be-gone, and save from death thy soul !    ere that false

word     be thine,     a    fa-ther's ma - le - dic     -     tion!

pp sotto voce assai.
Oh, fa - ther stern, thy curse too rash hath kill'd her like the lightning's
pp
Oh, fa - ther stern, thy curse too rash hath kill'd her like the lightning's
pp
Oh, fa - ther stern, thy curse too rash hath kill'd her like the lightning's
pp
Oh, fa - ther stern, thy curse too rash hath kill'd her like the lightning's
pp
Oh, fa - ther stern, thy curse too rash hath kill'd her like the lightning's
pp sotto voce assai.
Oh, fa - ther stern, thy curse too rash hath kill'd her like the lightning's
pp
Oh, fa - ther stern, thy curse too rash hath kill'd her like the lightning's
pp
Oh, fa - ther stern, thy curse too rash hath kill'd her like the lightning's
pp

flash,      the      light - ning's      flash!

flash,      the      light - ning's      flash!

flash,      the      light - ning's      flash!

flash,      the      light - ning's      flash!

flash,      the      light - ning's      flash!

flash,      the      light - ning's      flash!

flash,      the      light - ning's      flash!

flash,      the      light - ning's      flash!

CLARA.
Ri - gid fate, thy wrath is end - ed,
Allegro vivace.
p
with this last most stern af - flic - ti - on; what more
f p
dread - ful can be - fall me than a fa - ther's
f p
ma - le - dic - tion? Heav'n, which knows I am not
guil - ty, in its turn will send re - dress,

then, oh fa - ther, thine to suf - fer, when this

heart re - pose will bless,................ then, oh fa - ther, yes,

thine to suf - fer, when this heart re - pose will bless, then,.....

........ oh fa - ther, yes, thine to suf - fer, when this heart re -

- pose will bless, when........... this heart re - pose...... will bless.                                                    I

She

Can      she      the     mur - d'rer  name?      why

why

She

Will     she      the     mur - d'rer  name?      why

Can      she      the     mur - d'rer  name?      why

She       is       no     mur - der - ess,       tho'

Hence,   and      re -    pent    your    crime      in

Who      did      the     mur -   der,    say?      can

Who      did      the     mur -   der,    say?      can

Who      did      the     mur -   der,    say?      can

*Allegro vivace.*

ff

am    not    guil -  ty!

is    not    guil -  ty!

not    re - veal    it?    if    not    the    crime    her

not    re - veal    it?    if    not    the    crime    her

not    re - veal    it?    if    not    the    crime    her

she    con - ceal    it,    those    looks    of    in - no -

dark    se - clu - sion,    while    yet    on    earth    there's

you    re - veal......    it?    were    not    the    crime    your

you    re - veal    it?    were    not    the    crime    your

you    re - veal    it?    were    not    the    crime    your

by     Heav'n   I   swear,......................................

by     Heav'n   I   'swear,....................................

. own,.    why    thus   con - ceal ?........................

own,    why    thus   con - ceal it? yes, were not the . crime her own

. .own,   : why    thus .. con - ceal it ? yes, were not the : crime her own

. . ceuce,..    .plain - - ly   re - veal it, oh,· pi - ty. her ; sor - . rows,

time;    ere    life's ' con - clu-sion fly, ' fly from man - kind, and fly

. own, ·· would'    you   con - ceal...............  -     it?............

own,    would    you ' con - ceal ··   it ? · ·

: own,    · would    you   con - ceal it ? yes, were not the · crime your own,

I am no mur-der-ess, tho' I con - ceal it! I swear.........

she is no mur-der-ess, tho' she con - ceal it! I swear.........

if not the crime her own, why thus con - ceal it? ah, why?.........

why thus con - ceal........., it?............. were not, yes,

why thus con - ceal........., it?............. were not, yes,

Thou who canst aid............. them,............. pi - ty, oh,

to dark se - clu - - - - - sion,............. and when to

if not the crime your own, would you con - ceal it? and why?.........

were not the crime yours

would you con - ceal........., it?............. no more dis -

8va.........

I am no mur - der - ess

she is no mur - der - ess

if not the crime her own

were not the crime her own, why thus con - ceal...............

were not the crime her own, why thus con - ceal...............

pi - ty her sor - rows, Thou who canst aid,...............

death con - sign'd, peace may you find, may you find,...............

were not the crime your own,

why thus

- sem - ble, hence, hence from this clois - ter, and re - - - - - - - -

8va...................................

tho' I con - ceal it, no, no, I am no mur - der - ess, I

tho' she con - ceal it, no, no, she is no mur - der - ess, no,

why thus con - ceal it? ah, why, why thus con - ceal, why thus con -

it? why thus con - ceal the mur - d'rer's name? why thus con -

it? why thus con - ceal the mur - d'rer's name? why thus con -

them, oh, pi - ty her, soothe her heart's pain, soothe her heart's

peace may you find, peace may you find, peace may you

why thus con - ceal it? ah, why, why thus con - ceal the mur - d'rer's

con - - ceal it? ah, why, why thus con - ceal the mur - d'rer's

- pent, re - pent your crime, re - pent your crime, re - pent your

The Royal Edition.—" The Siege of Rochelle."—(145)

I.

swear,    by    heav'n,    I    swear!

no,    no,    no,    no,    no!

- ceal    the    mur - d'rer's    name?

- ceal?    why    thus    con - ceal?

- ceal?    why    thus    con - ceal?

pain,    soothe    her .    heart's    pain!

find,    peace    may    you    find!

name?    the    mur - d'rer's    name?

name?    the    mur - d'rer's    name?

crime,    re - pent    your    crime!

pp sotto voce.

I am no mur - der - ess, tho' I con - ceal.......

pp

She is no mur - der - ess, tho' she con - ceal.......

pp

Can she the mur - d'rer name? why not re - veal.......

pp

Can she the mur - d'rer name? why not re - veal.......

pp

Can she the mur - d'rer name? why not re - veal.......

pp

She is no mur - der - ess, tho' she con - ceal.......

pp

Hence, and re - pent your crime in dark se - clu -

p

it; these looks of in - no - cence plain - ly re -

it; those looks of in - no - cence plain - ly re -

it? if not the crime her own, why thus con -

it? if not the crime her own, why thus con -

it? if not the crime her own, why thus con -

it; those looks of in - no - cence plain - ly re -

- sion; while yet on earth there's time, ere life's con -

- veal....... it; pi - ty my sor - rows, Thou

- veal....... it; pi - ty her sor - rows, Thou

- ceal....... it? does she dis - sem - ble? and

ceal....... it? does she dis - sem - ble? and

- ceal....... it? does she dis - sem - ble? and

- veal it; pi - ty her sor - rows, Thou

- clu - sion; fly, fly from man - kind to

who.... canst aid....... them; saints of com-pas - - sion,

who.... canst aid....... them; saints of com-pas - - sion,

from.... what im - pulse? how her limbs trem - - ble,

from.... what im - pulse? how her limbs trem - - ble,

from.... what im - pulse? how her limbs trem - - ble,

who.... canst aid........ them; saints of com-pas - - sion,

dark se - clu - sion, and when to death........ con-sign'd,

soothe my heart's pain,......... saints of com - pas -

soothe her heart's pain,......... saints of com - pas -

'tis the heart's pain,......... how her limbs trem -

'tis the heart's pain,......... how her limbs trem -

'tis the heart's pain,......... how her limbs trem -

soothe her heart's pain,......... saints of com - pas -

peace may you find,......... and when to death

- - sion, saints of com - pas-sion, saints, soothe my heart's pain, my heart's pain;

- - siou, saints of com - pas- sion, saints, soothe her heart's pain, her heart's pain;

- - ble, how her limbs trem-ble, yes, 'tis the heart's pain, the heart's pain;

- - ble, how her limbs trem-ble, yes, 'tis the heart's pain, the heart's pain;

- - ble, how her limbs trem-ble, yes, 'tis the heart's pain, the heart's pain;

- - sion, saints of com - pas -sion, saints, soothe her heart's pain, her heart's pain;

........ consign'd, and when to death consign d, peace may you find, may you find;

Hence,

Hence,

Hence,

*cresc.*

*ff*

saints

saints

how

how

how

saints

ere

and re - pent your crime in se - clu - - -

and re - pent your crime in se - clu - -

and re - pent your crime in se - clu - -

of com - pas- sion,

of com - pas- sion,

her limbs trem-ble,

her limbe trem-ble,

her limbs trem-ble,

of com - pas-sion,

life's con - clu-sion,

- sion, while yet on earth there's time, ere

- sion, while yet on earth there's time, ere

- sion, while yet on earth there's time, ere

soothe my heart's pain; no, I am no mur-der-ess

soothe her heart's pain: no, she is no mur-der-ess

'tis the heart's pain; oh, can she the mur-d'rer name,

'tis the heart's pain; oh, can she the mur-d'rer name,

'tis the heart's pain!

soothe the heart's pain!

hence to re-pent; yes, hence, to re-pent your crime

life'e con-clu-sion re-pent!

life's con-clu-sion re-pent!

life's con-clu-sion re-pent!

tho' I con - ceal it, these looks of in - no - cence plain - ly re - veal it;

tho' she con - ceal it, those looks of in - no - cence plain - ly re - veal it;

why not re - veal it? if not the crime her own, why thus con - ceal it?

why not re - veal it? if not the crime her own, why thus con - ceal it?

ere life's con - clu - sion, while yet on earth there's time, in dark se - clu - sion, pi - ty my sor-rows, oh. saints, pi - ty me,         pi -

pi - ty her sor-rows, oh, saints, pi - ty her,        pi -

why thus con - ceal it? ah, why thus con - ceal?       why

why thus con - ceal it? ah, why thus con - ceal?      why thus con -

why thus con - ceal     the     mur-der-er's

saints, pi - ty her,     and     soothe her heart's

fly from man-kind, yes, fly, fly from man-kind,     fly from man-

fly from man - kind,     hence,

fly from man-kind,     hence,     fly from man -

fly from man-kind,     hence,     fly from man -

*cresc.*    *f*

ty,                          pi - ty!

ty,                          pi - ty!

thus                         con - - ceal?

- ceal                       the murd'rer's name?

name?        yes,        the        mur-der-er's name?

pain,        saints,        soothe,        soothe her heart's pain!

- kind,                      fly from man - kind!

hence,        fly from man - kind,        hence,        hence,        fly from man -

- kind,        hence,        hence,        fly from man - kind,...................

- kind,        hence,        hence,        fly from man - kind,...................

kind to dark se - clu - sion, and when to death consign'd, peace may you

and when to death consign'd, peace may you

and when to death consign'd, peace may you

I am no mur - der - ess, tho' I con - ceal.......

She is no mur - der - ess, tho' she con - ceal.......

Can she the mur - d'rer name? why not re - veal.......

Can she the mur - d'rer name? why not re - veal.......

Can she the mur - d'rer name? why not re - veal.......

She is no mur - der - ess, tho' she con - ceal.......

Hence, and re - pent your crime in dark se - clu -

find, in death, peace may you

find, in death, peace may you

find, in death, peace may you

it; these looks of in - no - cence plain - ly re -

it; those looks of in - no - cence plain - ly re -

it? if not the crime her own, why thus con -

it? if not the crime her own, why thus con -

it? if not the crime her own, why thus con -

it; those looks of in - no - cence plain - ly re -

- sion; while yet on earth there's time, ere life's con -

find, hence, hence and

find, hence, hence and

find, hence, hence and

-veal....... it; pi - ty my sor - rows; Thou

-veal....... it; pi - ty her sor - rows, Thou

- ceal....... it? does she dis - sem - ble? and

- ceal....... it? does she dis - sem - ble? and

- ceal....... it? does she dis - sem - ble? and

- veal it; pi - ty her sor - rows, Thou

- clu - sion; fly, fly from man - kind to

re - pent!

re - pent!

re - pent!

who.... canst aid....... them; saints of com - pas - - sion,

who.... canst aid....... them; saints of com - pas - - sion,

from.... what im - pulse? how her limbs trem - - ble,

from.... what im - pulse? how her limbs trem - - ble,

from.... what im - pulse? how her limbs trem - - ble,

who.... canst aid....... them; saints of com - pas - - sion,

dark se - clu - - sion, and when to death con - sign'd,

soothe my heart's pain,......... saints of com - pas -

soothe her heart's pain,......... saints of com - pas -

'tis the heart's pain,......... how her limbs trem -

'tis the heart's pain,......... how her limbs trem -

'tis the heart's pain,......... how her limbs trem -

soothe her heart's pain,......... saints of com - pas -

peace may you find,......... and when to death

and when to death

and when to death

and when to death

*più moto.*

- - sion, saints of com - pas-sion, saints, soothe my heart's pain, my heart's pain!

- - sion, saints of com - pas-sion, saints, soothe her heart's pain, her heart's pain!

- - ble, how her limbs trem-ble, yes, 'tis the heart's pain, the heart's pain!

- - ble, how her limbs trem-ble, yes, 'tis the heart's pain, the heart's pain, how she

- - ble, how her limbs trem-ble, yes, 'tis the heart's pain, the heart's pain, how she

- - sion, saints of com - pas -sion, saints, soothe her heart's pain, her heart's pain, soothe her

con - sign'd, and when to death consign'd, peace may you find, may you find, when to

con - sign'd, peace may you find, and when to

con - sign'd, peace may you find, and when to

con - sign'd, peace may you find, and when to

*cresc.*

*ff*

how........... her

trem - bles, how her limbs trem - ble, 'tis the heart's pain, how

trem - bles, how her limbs trem - ble, 'tis the heart's pain, how

heart's pain, saints of com - pas - sion, soothe her heart's

death, when to death con - sign'd, peace may you find, peace may

death con - sign'd, when to death con - sign'd, peace may you find,

death con - sign'd, when to death con - sign'd, peace may you find,

death con - sign'd, when to death con - sign'd, peace may you find,

saints of com - pas - sion,.... soothe my heart's
saints of com - pas - sion,.... soothe her heart's
limbs...... trem - ble, 'tis the...... heart's pain,.... the heart's
she trem - bles, 'tis the...... heart's pain,.... the heart's
she trem - bles, 'tis the heart's pain,
pain, saints of com - pas - sion, soothe
you find, when to death con - sign'd
may........ you...... find,...... peace.... may...... you...... find,......
may you find, when to death con - sign'd,
may you find, when to death con - sign'd,

pain,...... soothe...... my........................................ heart's

pain,...... soothe.... her........................................... heart's

pain,...... 'tis...... .. the............. heart's..........

pain,...... 'tis........ .. the............. heart's..........

'tis............... the............... heart's..........

her heart's pain,........... soothe.........

peace may you............. find,.............

peace...... may...... you.............

peace...... may...... you............................................

peace...... may...... you............................................

8va..........

ff

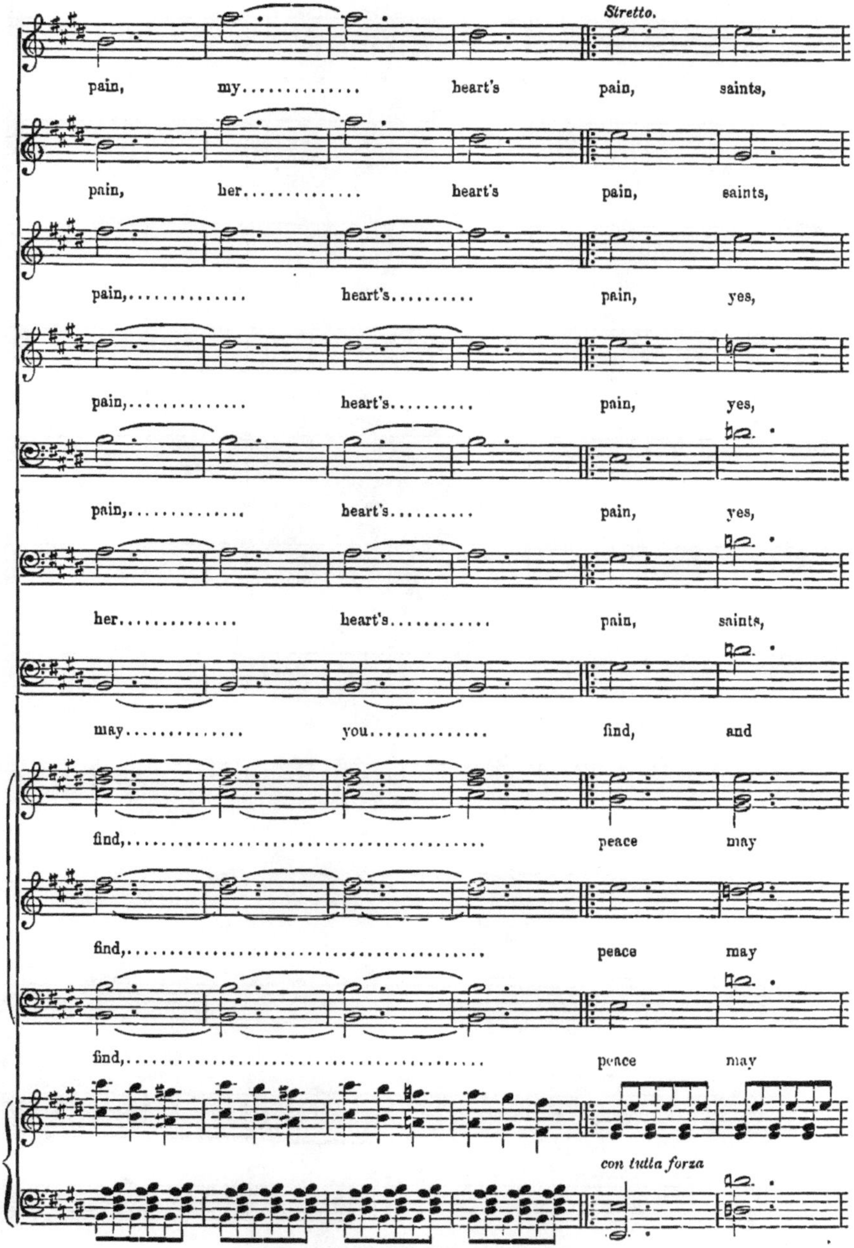
Stretto.
pain, my.............. heart's pain, saints,
pain, her.............. heart's pain, saints,
pain,.............. heart's.......... pain, yes,
pain,.............. heart's.......... pain, yes,
pain,.............. heart's.......... pain, yes,
her.............. heart's............ pain, saints,
may.............. you.............. find, and
find,.......................................... peace may
find,.......................................... peace may
find,.......................................... peace may
con tutta forza

soothe my heart's pain, soothe my heart's

soothe her heart's pain, soothe her heart's

'tis the heart's pain, 'tis the heart's

'tis the heart's pain, 'tis the heart's

'tis the heart's pain, 'tis the heart's

soothe her heart's pain, soothe her heart's

peace may you find, peace may you

you find, peace may...... you find,

you find, peace may...... you find,

you find, peace may...... you find,

pain, soothe my heart's pain, soothe

pain, soothe her heart's pain, soothe

pain, 'tis the heart's pain, 'tis

pain, 'tis the heart's pain, 'tis

pain, 'tis the heart's pain, 'tis

pain, soothe her heart's pain, soothe

find, peace may you find, peace

peace, peace may you find, peace

peace, peace may you find, peace

peace, peace may you find, peace

my ... heart's ... pain, ... soothe ... my ... heart's ... pain, ... my

her ... heart's ... pain, ... soothe ... her ... heart's ... pain, ... her

the ... heart's ... pain, ... 'tis ... the ... heart's ... pain, ... 'tis

the ... heart's ... pain, ... 'tis ... the ... heart's ... pain, ... 'tis

the ... heart's ... pain, ... 'tis ... the ... heart's ... pain, ... 'tis

her ... heart's ... pain, ... soothe ... her ... heart's ... pain, ... soothe

may ... you ... find, ... peace ... may ... you ... find, ... peace

may ... you ... find, ... peace ... may ... you ... find, ... peace

may ... you ... find, ... peace ... may ... you ... find, ... peace

may ... you ... find, ... peace ... may ... you ... find, ... peace

heart's, my heart's............................................ pain!

heart's, her heart's........................................... pain!

the heart's pain, 'tis the heart's pain, 'tis the heart's pain!

the heart's pain, 'tis the heart's pain, 'tis the heart's pain!

the heart's pain, 'tis the heart's pain, 'tis the heart's pain!

her heart's pain, soothe her heart's pain, soothe her heart's pain!

may you find, peace may you find, peace may you find!

may you find, peace may you find, peace may you find!

may you find, peace may you find, peace may you find!

may you find, peace may you find, peace may you find!

may you find, peace may you find, peace may you find!

END OF ACT I.

# ACT II.

## No. 10. CHORUS.

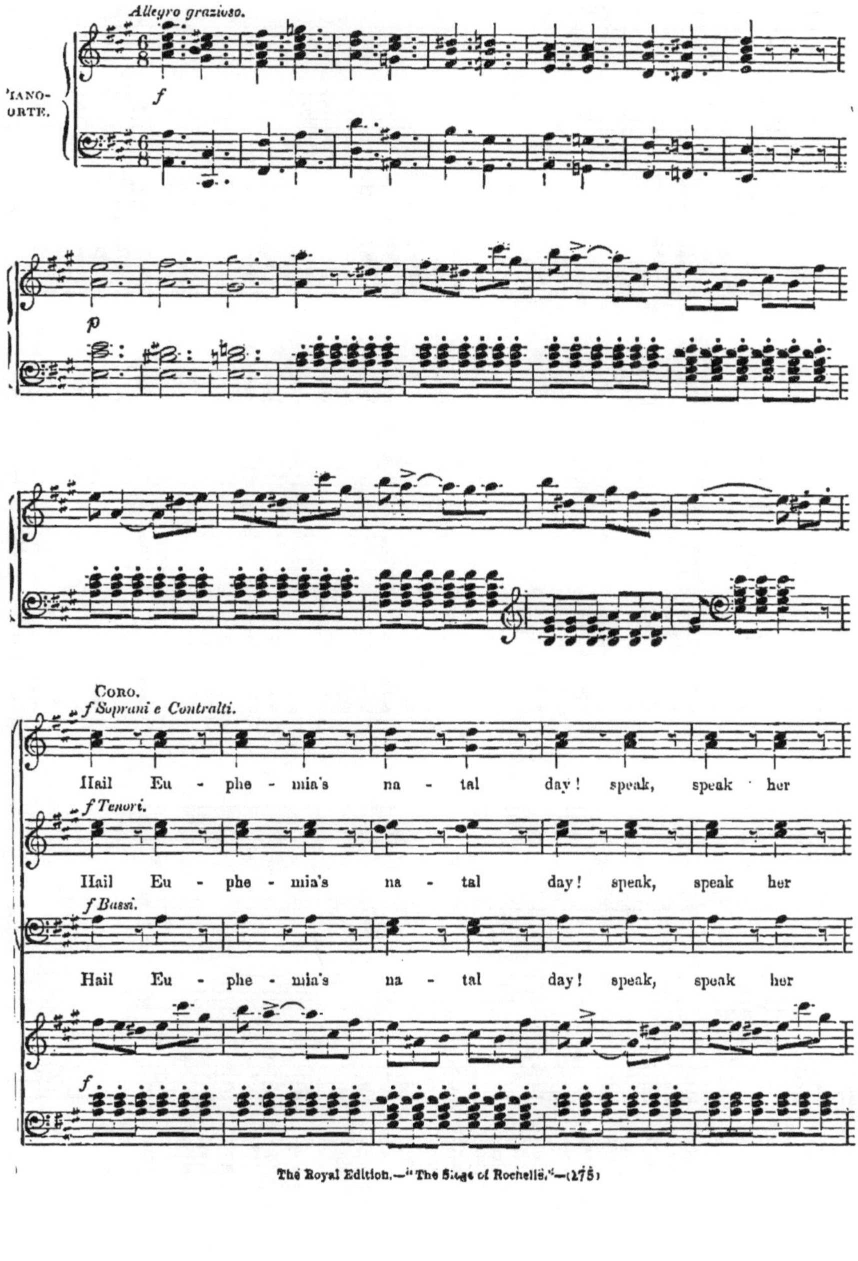

praises, ev - 'ry voice, ev - 'ry lip for

praises, ev - 'ry voice, ev - 'ry lip for

praises, ev - 'ry voice, ev - 'ry lip for

her must pray; yes, ev - 'ry breast with hers re -

her must pray; yes, ev - 'ry breast with hers re -

her must pray; yes, ev - 'ry breast with hers re -

- joice, re - joice, re - joice!

- joice, re - joice, re - joice! greet,

- joice, re - joice, re - joice! greet,

greet, greet with spright-ly dance the hour, ca-rol, birds, yes,

greet with spright-ly dance the hour, ca-rol, birds, your live-liest lay,

greet with spright-ly dance the hour, ca-rol, birds, your live-liest lay,

ca-rol, birds, your live-liest lay;

ca-rol, birds, your live-liest lay;

ca-rol, birds, your live-liest lay;

cresc.

cresc.
greet, with spright - ly, with
birds, ca - rol, birds, your live - liest, live - liest lay, greet, with spright - ly, with
birds, ca - rol, birds, your live - liest, live - liest lay, greet, with spright - ly, with
cresc.
spright- ly dance the hour, the hour; ca - rol, birds, ca - rol, birds, the live - liest,
spright- ly dance the hour, the hour; ca - rol, birds, ca - rol, birds, the live - liest,
spright- ly dance the hour, the hour; ca - rol, birds, ca - rol, birds, the live - liest,
live- liest lay; sweet - est per - fume clothe the bow - er,
live- liest lay; sweet - est per - fume clothe the bow - er,
live- liest lay; sweet - est per - fume clothe the bow - er,

'tis....... Eu - phe - mia's na - tal day! 'tis Eu - phe - mia's na - tal

'tis Eu - phe - mia's na - tal day! 'tis Eu - phe - mia's na - tal

'tis Eu - phe - mia's na - tal day! 'tis Eu - phe - mia's na - tal

day! 'tis Eu - phe - mia's na - tal day! Eu - phe - mia's na - tal

day! 'tis Eu - phe - mia's na - tal day! Eu - phe - mia's na - tal

day! 'tis Eu - phe - mia's na - tal day! Eu - phe - mia's na - tal

day! Hail Eu - phe - mia's

day! Hail Eu - phe - mia's

day! Hail Eu - phe - mia's

na - tal    day! speak,    speak her    prai - ses,    ev - 'ry

na - tal    day! speak,    speak her    prai - ses,    ev - 'ry

voice;    ev - 'ry    lip    for    her    must    pray, yes,

voice;    ev - 'ry    lip    for    her    must    pray, yes,

voice;    ev - 'ry    lip    for    her    must    pray, yes,

ev - 'ry    heart    with    hers    re - joice,    let    ev - 'ry

ev - 'ry    heart    with    hers    re - joice,    let    ev - 'ry

ev - 'ry    heart    with    hers    re - joice,    let    ev - 'ry

breast with hers re - joice, re - - joice, let
breast with hers re - joice, re - - joice, let
ev - 'ry breast with hers re - joice, re - -
ev - 'ry breast with hers re - joice, re - -
ev - 'ry breast with hers re - joice, re - -
- joice, let ev - 'ry breast with hers re - joice, let ev - 'ry
- joice, let ev - 'ry breast with hers re - joice, let ev - 'ry
- joice, let ev - 'ry breast with hers re - joice, let ev - 'ry

breast with hers re - joice, let ev - 'ry

breast with hers re - joice, let ev - 'ry

breast with hers re - joice, let ev - 'ry

breast with hers re - joice!...............

breast with hers re - joice!...............

breast with hers re - joice!...............

*pp sotto voce*

Lo, the sky with clouds en-

Lo, the sky with clouds en-

Lo, the sky with clouds en-

-man - - tled, shoots forth beams............ of an - gry

-man - - tled, shoots forth beams............ of an - gry

-man - tled, shoots forth beams............ of an - gry

light!............ hark! now dis - tant thun - der

light!............ hark! now dis - tant thun - der

light!............ hark! now dis - tant thun - der

peal - ing, fills each bo - som with af - fright!

peal - ing, fills each bo - som with af - fright!

peal - ing, fills each bo - som with af - fright!

*cresc.*

*ff*

see, too, how the fu - rious

*ff*

see, too, how the fu - rious

*ff*

see, too, how the fu - rious

*8va........*

*ff*

wa - - - ters lash the

wa - - - ters lash the

wa - - - ters lash the

*8va........*

shore with sil - v'ry, sil - v'ry spray; lo, what

shore with sil - v'ry, sil - v'ry spray; lo, what

shore with sil - v'ry, sil - v'ry spray; lo, what

8va..................

form comes thro' the tem - - - - pest

form comes thro' the tem - - - - pest

form comes thro' the tem - - - - pest

8va..................

like the spi - rit of........ dis - may!

like the spi - rit of........ dis - may

like the spi - rit of........ dis - may!

8va..................

CLARA. (*Behind the scenes.*)

Aid me! aid me!

hark! hark!

hark! hark!

hark! hark!

hark! what means that trem-bling cry, that tone of hu-man

hark! what means that trem-bling cry, that tone of hu-man

hark! what means that trem-bling cry, that tone of hu-man

pain, of hu - man

pain, of hu - man

pain, of hu - man

Aid.................. me!

pain? list-en, list-en, there...... a-

pain? list-en, list-en, there...... a-

pain? list-en, list-en, there...... a-

*f*

aid............................................ me!

-gain, lis-ten, lis-ten, there....... a-

-gain, lis-ten, lis-ten, there....... a-

-gain, lis-ten, lis-ten, there....... a-

-gain, through the storm that cry,............. I

-gain, through the storm that cry,............. I

-gain, through the storm that cry,............. I

*decresc.*

hear it still more near, thro' the storm that

hear it still more near, thro' the storm that

hear it still more near, thro' the storm that

cry,............... I · hear it still more near.

cry,............... I hear it still more near.

cry,............... I hear it still more near.

*pp*

Ped.

CLARA.

Aid me!

*pp*

aid me, or I die,........ aid me,

aid me, or I die, or...... I die!.................................

*sempre dim.*

........

No. 11.    Larghetto.    SONG.

PIANO-
FORTE.    dolce

MARCELLA.

One lit-tle kiss from lips I love, in the qui-et shade of our

na-tive grove is dear-er, far more dear to me, than all this

pomp... I see,..... than all this pomp I see.........................

Allegretto.

When the mer-ry, mer-ry dance pre-vails, and · twi-light tells no tales, no tales, when the mer-ry, mer-ry dance pre-vails, and twi-light tells no tales,

lit-tle kiss, 'tis not a-miss, no, no, no, no, no, no, no, no, no, no, no, no, 'tis

not a-miss, 'tis not a-miss, when the mer-ry, mer-ry dance pre-vails, and

twi-light tells no tales, no tales, when the mer-ry, mer-ry dance pre-vails, and

*cresc.*

twi-light tells................ no tales.

*f    ff*

*f*

Larghetto.

Hath gild-ed splen-dour such re-wards as the plea-sure which hum-ble

love ac-cords? one low-ly heart, one heart sin-cere out-vies, out-

vies.... each trea-sure here, each trea-sure here.....................

Allegretto.

When the mer-ry, mer-ry dance pre-vails, and twi-light tells no tales, no tales,

when the mer-ry, mer-ry dance pre-vails, and twi-light tells no tales,

lit - tle kiss, 'tis not a - miss, no, no, no, no, no, no, no, no, no, no, no, no, 'tis

not a-miss, 'tis not a - miss, when the mer - ry, mer - ry dance pre-vails, and

twi-light tells no tales, no tales, when the mer-ry, mer-ry dance pre-vails, and

*cresc.*

twi-light tells................... no tales.

*f*  *ff*  *f*

. 12.　　　　　　　CHORUS.

The Royal Edition.—"The Siege of Rochelle."—(194)

-ter, long life, long life to our no - ble, no-ble mas - ter;

-ter, long life, long life to our no - ble, no-ble mas - ter;

-ter, long life, long life to our no - ble, no-ble mas - ter;

fill, fill, with shouts the hall,

fill, fill, with shouts the hall,

fill, fill, with shouts the hall,

fill, fill with shouts the hall,

fill, fill with shouts the hall,

fill, fill with shouts the hall,

and his no - ble, no - ble guest;

and his no - ble, no - ble guest;

and his no - ble, no - ble guest;

wel - come, wel - come............. all, yes,

wel - come, wel - come, wel - come all,

wel - come, wel - come, wel - come all,

wel - come, wel - come, wel - - come all;

wel - come, wel - come, wel - - come all;

long life, long life to our no - ble, our no - ble mas -

long life, long life to our no - ble, our no - ble mas -

long life, long life to our no - ble, our no - ble mas -

- ter, long life, long life to our no - ble, no - ble mas - ter;

- ter, long life, long life to our no - ble, no - ble mas - ter;

- ter, long life, long life to our no - ble, no - ble mas - ter;

fill, fill with shouts the hall, for our dear mas - ter;

fill, fill with shouts the hall, for our dear mas - ter;

fill, fill with shouts the hall, for our dear mas - ter;

wel - come, yes, wel - come all, wel - come all,......................

wel - come, yes, wel - come all, wel - come all,......................

wel - come, yes, wel - come all, wel - come all,......................

...... wel - come all;...................... fill with shouts the

...... wel - come all;...................... fill with shouts the

...... wel - come all;...................... fill with shouts the

hall; wel - - come, wel - come all, wel - come
hall; wel - - come, wel - come all, wel - come
hall; wel - come, wel - come, wel - come all, wel - come
all, wel - come all, wel - come all, wel - come all!
all, wel - come all, wel - come all, wel - come all!
all, wel - come all, wel - come all, wel - come all!

# ROMANCE.

When I be - held the an - chor weigh'd, and with the shore thine

im - age fade, I deem'd each wave a bound - less sea that bore me still from love and thee; I watch'd a-lone the sun de-cline, and en-vied beams on thee to

shine,...... while..................... an-guish paint-ed 'neath her spell, my

love and cottage near Ro-chelle,.... my love and cot-tage near.... Ro-

-chelle, my love...... and cot-tage near Ro-chelle, near................. Ro-

-chelle.                                                    'Mid

ev -'ry clime would mem'-ry trace in ev -'ry scene that gen - tle face. that

mute pale lip, thy part - ing sigh, that one sad tear which fill'd thine eye,      'till

fan - cy's dream   with sweet con - trol        on   ma - gic wings would lift my soul,...... and.................. ........ waft me home with ye to dwell, my

love and cot-tage near Ro - chelle,.... my love and cot - tage near.... Ro -

- chelle, my love....... and cot - tage near Ro - chelle, near............... Ro -

- chelle.

No. 14.

# TRIO.

*Moderato.* RECIT.                    ROSENBERG.

Who art thou? thy mission
say.                                                    Mon-

MONTALBAN.

Ro - sen - berg,

- tal - ban,  soon I'll fol - low;        yes,    thou would'st re-move her?

she  is  here,  Cla - ra.

MONTALBAN.

This  ve - ry hour:  give me but  mo - ney,  with  her  I'll  seek  the  In - dies;

ROSENBERG.

nev-er more her presence shall af-flict you. But how to quit the pa-lace? it must be un-ob-

*fp*

MONTALBAN.

-serv'd. A boat is on the riv-er; a trus-ty ser-vant to row us half a

*fp*

Such a one I have, Mi-chel!

league would be suf-fi-cient. In the night's dark-ness,

*fp*

while the fête pre-vails, if she re-fuse to fol-low, force shall aid me; keep Val-

*fp*     *fp*

ROSENBERG.

-mour from the spot; but this ser-vant, where is he? Mi-chel!

ho! Mi-chel! you will o-bey his

(pointing to Montalban.)    Allegro moderato.

or-ders, I com-mand you.

MICHEL.    ROSENBERG.

I shall do, sir, as you re-quire me. Yes, you may

MICHEL.

trust him." (The cub of Sa-tan, his looks be-tray him; he's

plot - ting some mischief.) Well! I shall do, sir, what you de - sire me.

MONTALBAN.

Be this mo - ment rea - dy!

Nev - er fear.

ROSENBERG.

He is brave and stea - dy.

If you

please, sir, your commands I would hear,

I would hear.

ROSENBERG.

Show all o -

- be - dience; your mas - ter see.

MICHEL.

My mas - ter!

he no mas-ter is to me. No doubt.
ROSENBERG.
He is, sir, a gen-tle-man. You'll him o-
-bey, sir, as 'twere me, or of-fend-ed I shall
All my best I'll try, but—
ROSENBERG.
be. Nought must in-ter-vene;
MONTALBAN.
Nought must in-ter-vene;
cou-rage! cou-rage! cou-rage and fi-de-li-ty!
cou-rage! cou-rage! cou-rage and fi-de-li-ty!
ff

MICHEL.

(Cou - rage! cou - rage! cou - rage and fi - de - li - ty! what on

earth can they mean? what on earth can they mean?

Cou - rage and fi - de - li - ty! cou - rage and fi - de - li -

Cou - rage and fi - de - li - ty! cou - rage and fi - de - li -

Cou - rage and fi - de - li - ty! cou - rage and fi - de - li -

- ty!)

- ty!

- ty!

MONTALBAN.

On the riv - er, near the

cha - pel, when the shades of night de - scend, 'neath the wil - low which screens yon

MICHEL.

wa - ter, in a boat you must at - tend. In that boat at such an

hour, to whom must I as - sist - ance lend?

Your task, sir, is the oar to

Your task, sir, is the oar to

But—

ply. Nought must in - ter - vene; si - lence! si - lence!

ply. Nought must in - ter - vene; si - lence! si - lence!

MICHEL.
si - lence and fi - de - li - ty! (Si - lence! si - lence!
si - lence and fi - de - li - ty!
p
si - lence and fi - de - li - ty! what on earth can this im -
- ply? what on earth can this mean? Well, 'tis my du - ty, I o -
8va
p
- bey, tho' from the fête to keep a - way pla - guy hard 'tis, all so

gay; and my wife, too, and my wife, too, she will

ROSENBERG.

cry, yes!) O - be - dience and fi - de - li - ty,

MONTALBAN.

O - be - dience and fi - de - li - ty,

gold a re - com - pence will buy.

MICHEL.

(O - be - dience and fi -

- de - li - ty! what on earth can they mean?)

Andante.      *dulce.*

*pp*

MONTALBAN.

(While........ the guests are i — — — dly

danc - ing, I............ the guil - ty girl........................ will

*cresc.*

seek;     if........... she dare....... re - sist........... my

*pp*

man - date,    vain........... each trem -bling pray'r, scornful word, or tear of

woe,...... force as - sist - ing if re - sist - - - -
- ing,........ from this...... man - sion she must go,...... she must
ff
p
pp
(What.......... they plot I'm half............... sus -
(At the noise of mu - sic
go! While the guests are i - dly
- pect - ing, by............ that ser - pent's gloo - - my
sound - ing, 'mid the hum of re - vel
danc - ing, I the guil - ty girl will

sneer; but.......... should Cla - ra need........... pro -

gay, na - - ture plead - ing, heart....... ex -

seek; force........ as - sist - ing

- tec - tion, she........... shall find........... it ev - - er

- ceed - ing, from....... this man - sion she.......... must

if.......... re - sist - ing, yes, she........... must

here, yes, be - tide me weal or woe,,....... yes, be - tide........ me, be -

go, yes, she must

go, force as - sist - ing if re - sist - - ing, from.......... this

- tide me weal or....... woe; sor - row heed - ing, wo - man's
go, she must go, yes,
man - sion she..... must.... go, force as - sist - ing if re -
ff
plead - ing, I'll.......... pro - tect where - e'er...... I........
yes, she........... must go, she must go, she must
- sist - ing, from.......... this man - sion.... she...... must....
go,.... where - e'er.... I...... go,.... where - e'er.... I......
go, yes, she must go, yes, she must
go,..... yes,.... she.... must.... go,..... yes,.... she.... must....

go,........ yes,........ I'll pro - tect........ where - e'er........... I

go,........ from........ this man - sion she........... must

go,........ from........ this man - sion she........... must

Allegro.

go.) Ev - er,

go.)

go.) You'll do your du-ty? be -

dim. pp

oh, nev - er.

My ser-vant brave and faith - ful, in zeal ne'er de -

- tray me?

The hon - our,

- fi - cient, this purse take, this purse take.

this purse take.

the honour is suf - fi - cient, ex - cuse the re - buff, the hon - our's e -

- nough.

Si - - - - - - -

Si - - - - - - -

ff

ff

aid - ing, the sail I'll soon be spread - ing, and time's on the wing;

aid - ing, the night is dim - ly shad - ing, and time's on the wing;

aid - ing, the night is dim - ly shad - ing, and time's on the wing;

*pp* hence. Mi - chel, de - lay not, yes, time is on the

*pp* fly, Mi - chel, de - lay not, yes, time is on the

*pp* fly, Mi - chel, de - lay not, yes, time is on the

*p*

wing, yes, time's on...... the wing, yes, time....... is on the

wing, yes, time's on...... the wing, yes, time....... is on the

wing, yes, time's on...... the wing, yes, time....... is on the

*cresc.* *ff.*

wing, yes, time.......... is on the wing,..... yes, time is on the

wing, yes, time.......... is on the wing...... yes, time is on the

wing, yes, time.......... is on the wing,..... yes, time is on the

wing, time's on the wing; haste, Mi - chel,

wing, time's on the wing; haste, Mi - chel,

wing, time's on the wing; haste, Mi - chel,

haste, Mi - chel, de - lay not, de -

haste, Mi - chel, de - lay not, de -

haste, Mi - chel, de - lay not, de -

-lay not, for time...... is on the wing, for time...... is on the

-lay not, for time...... is on the wing, for time...... is on the

-lay not, for time...... is on the wing, for time...... is on the

wing,............... for time is on the wing, is

wing,............... for time is on the wing, is

wing,............... for time is on the wing, is

on the wing. The twi-light now de -

on the wing. The twi-light now de -

on the wing. The twi-light now de -

- scend-ing, its gloo-my aid is lend - ing, per - haps this pro - ject end - ing, the

- scend-ing, its friend-ly aid is lend - ing, quick, quick, our pro - ject end - ing, the

- scend-ing, its gloo-my aid is lend - ing, quick, quick, our pro - ject end - ing, the

boat I'll quick - ly bring, the night is dim - ly shad - ing, the

boat in si - lence bring, the sail be wide - ly spread - ing, the

boat in si - lence bring, the sail be wide - ly spread - ing, the

breeze our flight is aid - ing, the sail I'll soon be spread - ing, for

breeze our flight is aid - ing, the night is dim - ly shad - ing, and

breeze our flight is aid - ing, the night is dim - ly shad - ing, and

The Royal Edition.—" The Siege of Rochelle."—(223)

time's on the wing; hence, Mi - chel, de - lay not,
time's on the wing; fly, Mi - chel, de - lay not,
time's on the wing; fly, Mi - chel, de - lay not,
p
yes, time is on the wing,...... yes, time's on........ the
yes, time is on the wing,...... yes, time's on........ the
yes, time is on the wing,...... yes, time's on........ the
f
ff
wing, yes, time........ is on the wing, yes, time........... is on the
wing, yes, time........ is on the wing, yes, time........... is on the
wing, yes, time........ is on the wing, yes, time........... is on the

wing........ yes, time is on the wing, time's on the

wing,........ yes, time is on the wing, time's on the

wing,........ yes, time is on the wing, time's on the

_pp poco più mosso._

wing; haste, Mi - chel, haste, Mi - chel,

wing; fly, Mi - chel,........... fly, Mi-chel,...........

wing; fly, Mi-chel,........... fly, Mi-chel,...........

haste, haste, Mi - chel, for time, for time.... is...... on...... the....

fly, fly, Mi - chel, for time, for time.... is...... on..... the....

fly, fly, Mi - chel, for time is on the

wing,　　　haste, Mi - chel,　　　　　haste, Mi - chel,

wing, fly, Mi - chel,..........　　fly, Mi - chel,............

wing, fly, Mi - chel,..........　　fly, Mi - chel,............

*pp*

haste,　　haste,　　Mi - chel, for time,　for　time　is...... on ... the....

haste,　　haste,　　Mi - chel, for time,　for　time　is...... on.... the....

fly,　　fly,　　Mi - chel,　for　　time　is　　on　　the

wing,　　haste, Mi - chel, for time, for　time　is　　on　　the

wing,　　fly, Mi - chel, for time, for　time　is　　on　　the

wing,　　fly, Mi - chel, for time, for　time　is　　on　　the

*ff*

wing, haste, Mi - chel, for time, for time is on the

wing, haste, Mi - chel, for time, for time is on the

wing, haste, Mi - chel, for time, for time is on the

wing, for time.... is on the wing, for time.... is on the wing, for time....

wing, for time.... is on the wing, for time.... is on the wing, for time....

wing, for time.... is on the wing, for time.... is on the wing, for time....

........ is on the wing.

........ is on the wing.

........ is on the wing.

# AIR.

'Twas in that gar-den beau-ti-ful, be-side the rose-tree bow'r, .... thy

gen-tle child had guile-less stray'd, to pluck for me a flow'r; I

heard, a-las, his fee-ble scream, and flew some fear to

chide, his lit - tle breast was stain'd with blood, in these sad arms he

died! his lit - tle breast was stain'd with blood, in these sad

arms he died!

You found my rai - ment dyed with gore, a dag - ger near me lay,........ I

saw the man who struck the blow, his name I dare not say! the dread - ful se - cret still...... to guard, my du - ty is I

feel, and let me suf - fer as I may, the grave my oath shall

seal! and let me suf - fer as I may, the grave my oath shall

seal!

# No. 16.

# DUET

tells the still - est hour, the still - est hour, when the

night - in - gale a - lone sad - ly tells the still - est hour,

wilt thou, wilt thou meet me, wilt thou meet me once a -

- gain,.... with the tear - drop, the tear - drop in thine eye? and the

look which speak - eth si - lent - ly the last, the last good - bye?.... and the

Lyrics under the music staves:

look.... which speak-eth si - lent - ly, the last,...... the last good....

bye, the look which speak - eth the

last good - bye? the look which

speak - eth the last good - bye?....................

...... the last good - bye?........................... the last............. good -

pp Clara.
- bye?
When the mer - ry strain, the
f
pp
pp
mer - ry strain is o'er which dis - tracts each ach - ing
heart, each heart, when the mu - sic, when the
mu - sic sounds no more I will meet thee but to
part, yes, but to part, when the mu - sic sounds no

more I will meet thee but to part; thou must breathe no

word,...... thou must breathe no word to me........ or ex - pect no

sad, no....... sad.... re - ply, but the look which speak - eth

si - lent-ly, the last, the last good - bye,.... but the look.... which speak-eth

si - lent-ly, the last,...... the last good - bye, the

look   which speak - eth   the   last      good -

- bye,          the   look      which  speak - eth   the

last         good - bye,...................... the last good -

- bye,.......................................... the last,      the

Oft the bright - est flow'rs de - cay,

Win-t'ry mists ob-sure the plain, but the cloud will pass a-way

but the cloud will pass a-way

and the spring flow'r bloom a - gain, the spring flow'r

and the spring flow'r bloom a - - gain, the spring flow'r

bloom a - - gain, and the spring flow'r bloom a -

bloom a - - gain, and the spring flow'r bloom a -

_cresc._

- gain, and the spring flow'r bloom a - gain.

*animato assai.*

- gain, and the spring flow'r bloom a - gain. Then for

love there sure is hope,.... and the hope that shall not die tho' our

hearts but fal - ter si - lent-ly their last, their last good bye ; then for

love there sure is hope,.... and the hope which shall not die tho' our

Then for love there sure is

hearts but mur - mur si - lent - ly, their last, their last good bye.

*cresc.*      *f*      *p*

hope,.... and the hope which shall not die tho' our hearts but fal - ter

si - lent - ly their last, their last good - bye; then for love there sure is

hope,..... and the hope which shall not die tho' our heart but fal - ter

VALMOUR.

si - lent - ly their last, their last good - bye. Yes, tho' our hearts but fal - ter

$f$   $ff$

si - lent - ly their last, their last good - bye, their last good -

CLARA.

Ah, Val - mour!

- bye; yes, still the clouds will pass a, -

- way,...... and the spring flow'r bloom a - gain, yes, bloom a -

CLARA. *with enthusiasm.*

Heav'ns! then for love there sure is hope,.... and the hope which shall not

- gain; then for love there sure is hope,.... and the hope which shall not

die tho' our hearts both fal - ter si - lent-ly their last, their last good -

die tho' our hearts both fal - ter si - lent-ly their last, their last good -

- bye; then for love there sure is hope,..... and the hope which shall not

- bye; then for love there sure is hope,..... and the hope which shall not

die tho' our hearts but fal - ter si - lent-ly their last, their last good -

die tho' our hearts but fal - ter si - lent-ly their last, their last good -

p
-bye, tho' our hearts but fal - ter si - lent-ly their last, their last good -
p
-bye, tho' our hearts but fal - ter si - lent-ly their last, their last good -
3 3 3 3
p
cresc.
-bye, tho' our hearts but fal - ter their last good -
cresc.
f
-bye, tho' our hearts but fal - ter their last good -
f
cresc.
f
p
-bye, tho' our hearts but fal - ter si - lent-ly their last, their last good -
p
-bye, tho' our hearts but fal - ter si - lent-ly their last, their last good -
p
cresc.
-bye, tho' our hearts but fal - - ter their
cresc.
-bye, tho' our hearts but fal - - ter their
cresc.

last good - bye, their last good - bye, their

last good - bye, their last good - bye, their

last good - bye, their last good - bye, their last good - bye, their

last good - bye, their last good - bye, their last good - bye, their

last good - bye.

last good - bye.

# DUET.

*Moderato.*

PIANO-
FORTE.

*ff*

ROSENBERG.

The feel - ing heart would thrill with woe......... nor ev - er

know, nor ev - er know a mo - ment's rest, as - sur'd too late it had con -

- demn'd,.... as - sur'd too late it had con-demn'd a guilt - less breast.

Heav'n! ere such re-morse my doom, my doom, of mem - 'ry be this brain be -

- reav'd, of mem - 'ry be this brain be - reav'd, ere too

late.......... con - vic - tion come,......... oh, let me die........ de -

- ceiv'd! oh, let me die de - ceiv'd! oh, let me

die, let me die de - ceiv'd! Her gen - tle truth, oh, had I

wrong'd,...... or could I think, or could I think thou'dst been mis-led, 'twere

o'er,........ 'twere bet-ter death my young life

bet - ter death my young life o'er,........ 'twere bet-ter death my young life o'er its

blight had shed ; Heav'n! ere such de-spair my doom, my doom, of

rea - son be this brain be - reav'd,

rea - son be this brain be - reav'd, of rea - son be this brain be -

-reav'd; ere too late............con-vic-tion come,.........oh, let me

die........ de - ceiv'd! oh, let me die de -

-ceiv'd! oh, let me die de - ceiv'd! The feel - - ing

*poco più mosso.* *p dolce.*

The feel - - ing

heart would thrill with woe nor ev - er know a mo - ment's rest, as -

heart would thrill with woe nor ev - er know a mo - ment's rest, as -

-sur'd too late it had con - demn'd a guilt - less
-sur'd too late it had con - demn'd a guilt - less
breast; Heav'n! ere such de - spair my doom, of rea - son be this
breast; Heav'n! ere such de - spair my doom,
brain be - reav'd,........ ere too late con - vic - tion comes, oh,
ere too late con - vic - tion comes, oh, let me die de -
let me die de - ceiv'd! oh, let me die de - ceiv'd! oh,
-ceiv'd! de - ceiv'd! oh, let me die de - ceiv'd! oh,

let me die de - ceiv'd! Heav'n! ere such re - morse my

let me die de - ceiv'd! Heav'n! ere such re - morse my

doom, of mem' - ry be this brain be-reav'd, ere too

doom, of mem' - ry be this brain be-reav'd, ere too

late con - vic - tion come, oh, let me die de - - ceiv'd! oh, let me

late con - vic - tion come, oh, let me die de - - ceiv'd! oh, let me

*più mosso.*

die,............. let me die........ de - ceiv'd! oh, let me die,.........

die,............. let me die........ de - ceiv'd! oh, let me die,.........

oh, let me die,.......... oh, let me die de - ceiv'd! oh, let me die,.......

oh, let me die,.......... oh, let me die de - ceiv'd! oh, let me die,.......

.... oh, let me die,.......... oh, let me die de - ceiv'd! let me

.... oh, let me die,.......... oh, let me die de - ceiv'd! let me

die, let me die de - ceiv'd!

die, let me die de - ceiv'd!

No. 18           DUET.

*Allegro vivace.*

PIANO-FORTE.

MICHEL.

Once a wolf, so fa - bles say, with hun-gry tooth and eyes of fire,

thought a harm-less lamb to slay, con-ceal'd be - neath, conceal'd be -

- neath a sheep's at - tire,..... con - ceal'd be - neath a..... sheep's at -

- tire,

but a shep - herd, sly sus - pect - ing,........ did a

cun-ning, did a cun-ning noose pre - pare; so sir wolf, when least ex -

- pect-ing, ... hung, sir, dangling, hung, sir, dangling in the air, then, sir wolf, when least sus-

- pect-ing, hung, sir, dangling in the air! but a shepherd, sly sus - pect-ing, did a cunning noose pre-

- pare, so sir wolf, when least sus-pect-ing, hung, sir, dangling in the air, hung, sir, dangling in the air, hung, sir, dang - ling, dang - ling in the air!

MONTALBAN.

Once a cur of mon-grel

breed presum'd a no - ble horse to bay, but one kick from that proud

steed, and in the mire the mon-grel lay, and in the mire.... the mon-grel

lay, the mon - grel lay;

how he howl'd dis-tort'd and maim'd, sir,...... roll-ing,

roll-ing in the mud, sir, there, with his dy-ing breath ex - claim-ing..... "Of the

heels, of the heels you'd bite, be-ware," with his dy-ing breath ex-claiming, "Of the heels you'd bite, be -

- ware;" how he howl'd, distort'd and maim'd, sir, roll-ing in the mud, sir, there, with his dy-ing breath ex -

- claim-ing, "Of the heels you'd bite, be - ware, of the heels you'd bite, be - ware, of the heels.......... you'd bite,..... be - ware!"

MICHEL.
Now, your

ser - vant, I am go - ing,

MONTALBAN.
stay! my man - ners ere I go. Have a care of me when

speak - ing; guard your tongue with cau - tious art.

MICHEL. MONTALBAN. MICHEL. MONTALBAN
You such pru - dence— Will re - pay, sir. If sus - pi - cion— You be -

MICHEL. MONTALBAN.

-tray, sir, then— What then? Then this dag-ger to your heart, then this dag-ger to your

heart! so be-gone, sir, I com-mand. now we each

o-ther un-der-stand. I o-bey, sir, your com-mand, sir, your com-

-mand; now we each o-ther

Now we each o-ther un-der-stand, now we each o-ther

un-der-stand, we each o-ther un-der-

un-der-stand, we each o-ther un-der

- stand, we each o - ther un - der - stand, we each o - ther un - der -

- stand, we each o - ther un - der - stand, we each o - ther un - der -

- stand, we each o - ther un - der - stand. Sir, an in-stant, if you

please; but one word ere I de - part. Speak! au -

MONTALBAN.

MICHEL.

- da - cions! 'Tis a se - cret,

MONTALBAN.

I would play a grate - ful part. Knave, what mean you?

MICHEL.

Don't, you fright me, don't, you fright me.

MONTALBAN.

You this dag - ger— Would re - quite, sir. How?

MICHEL.

oh! With two bul-lets for your heart, with two bul-lets for your heart! ha, ha, ha, ha,

so be-gone, sir, I com-mand, now we each o-ther un-der-stand.

MONTALBAN.                                    MICHEL.

Jus-tice I will quick de-mand,    I will de-mand,    Now we each o-ther un-der-stand,

........ now we each o - ther  un - der - stand,      we      each

MONTALBAN.

This I do not, sir, un - der - stand,        this      I

o - ther      un - - - der - stand,  we  each  o - ther  un - der -

do not      un - - - der - stand,  this  I  do  not un - der -

- stand, we  each  o - ther un - der - stand, we  each  o - ther un - der -

- stand, this  I  do  not un - der - stand, this  I  do  not un - der -

poco più mosso.
- stand, now be-gone, sir, I com-mand, we each o-ther un-der-stand, so be-gone, sir, I com -
- stand, jus-tice I will quick de-mand, this I do not un-der-stand, jus-tice I will quick de -
- mand, we each o-ther un-der-stand, we each o-ther un-der-stand, sir, we each o-ther un-der -
- mand, this I do not un-der-stand, this I do not un-der-stand, sir, this I do not un-der -
cresc.
- staud, we each o-ther, we each o-ther, we each o ther un-der-stand, so be-gone, sir, I com -
- stand, this I do not, this I do not, this I do not un-der-stand, jus-tice I will quick de -
- mand, we each o-ther un-der-stand, so be-gone, sir, I com-mand, we each o-ther un-der -
- mand, this I do not un-der-stand, jus-tice I will quick de-mand, this I do not un-der -

Soprano: stand, we each o-ther un-der-stand, sir, we each o-ther un-der-stand, we each o-ther, we each

Bass: stand, this I do not un-der-stand, sir, this I do not un-der-stand, this I do not, this I

Soprano: o-ther, we each o-ther un-der-stand, we each o-ther un-der-

Bass: do not, this I do not un-der-stand, this I do not un-der-

Soprano: stand, we each o-ther un-der-stand!

Bass: stand, this I do not un-der-stand!

No. 19. FINALE.

Allegro spirito.
CLARA.
Oh, hap - py
MARCELLA.
Oh, hap - py
VALMOUR.
Oh, hap - py
MICHEL.
Oh, hap - py
AZINO AND ROSENBERG.
Allegro spirito.
PIANO-FORTE.
mo - ment,...... a - way all sor - row,.... hence sighs and tear - drops...... un - til to -
mo - ment,...... a - way all sor - row,.... hence sighs and tear - drops...... un - til to -
mo - ment,...... a - way all sor - row,.... hence sighs and tear - drops...... un - til to -
mo - ment,...... a - way all sor - row,.... hence sighs and tear - drops...... un - til to -
Oh, hap - py mo - - ment, a - way all sor - -

- mor - row, joy's gold-en trans - ports,...... oh, let us bor - row,...... while yet the

- mor - row, joy's gold-en trans - ports,...... oh, let us bor - row,..... while yet the

- mor - row, joy's gold-en trans - ports,...... oh, let us bor - row,..... while yet the

- mor - row, joy's gold-en trans - ports,...... oh, let us bor - row,..... while yet the

- row, joy's gold-en trans - - ports,

sun of........... rap-ture shine, each past re - gret thus...... for ev - er

sun of........... rap-ture shine, each past re - gret thus...... for ev - er

sun of........... rap-ture shine, each past re - gret thus...... for ev - er

sun of.. ......... rap-ture shine,

oh, let us bor - - row,

end - ing,                                                          fame's daz - zling

end - ing,                                                          fame's daz - zling

end - ing,                                                          fame's daz - zling

fame's daz'- zling lus - tre...... a - round de - scend - ing,    fame's daz - zling

fame's daz - zling lus - tre...... a - round de - scend - ing,    fame's daz - zling

lus - - - tre        a - round de - scend - - -

lus - - - tre        a - round de - scend - - -

lus - - - tre        a - round de - scend - - -

lus - - - tre        a - round de - scend - - -

lus - - - tre        a - round de - scend - - -

-ing,     vic - to - ry   al   -   so      her bright aid lend - ing,

-ing,     vic - to - ry   al   -   so      her bright aid lend - ing,

-ing, vic - to - ry   al - so     her bright aid lend-ing,     the brave with

-ing, vic - to - ry   al - so     her bright aid lend-ing,     the brave with

-ing, vic - to - ry   al - so     her bright aid lend-ing,     the brave with

the brave with glo - ry's......... wreath en - twine,..............

the brave with glo - ry s......... wreath en - twine,..............

glo - ry,     the brave with glo-ry's wreath en - twine,..............

glo - ry,     the brave with glo-ry s wreath en - twine,     with

glo - ry,     the brave with glo-ry s wreath en - twine,     with en - - - twine, with glo - ry's wreath en -

en - - - twine, with glo - ry's wreath en -

en - - - twine, with glo-ry's wreath,.....................................

glo - ry's wreath, the brave with glo - ry's wreath en -

glo - ry's wreath, the brave with glo - ry's wreath en -

*Soprani e Contralti.*

With glo-ry's wreath,.....................................

*Tenori.*

The brave with glo - ry's wreath en -

*Bassi.*

The brave with glo - ry's wreath en -

- twine,     with     glo - ry's   wreath en - twine,..................

- twine,     with     glo - ry's   wreath en - twine,..................

.... with glo-ry's   wreath.......................... en - twine,..................

- twine,     the brave with   glo - ry's   wreath en - twine,   the brave    with

- twine,     the brave with   glo - ry's   wreath en - twine,   the brave    with

.... with glo-ry's   wreath.......................... en - twine,..................

- twine,     the brave with   glo - ry's   wreath en - twine,   the brave    with

- twine,     the brave with   glo - ry's   wreath en - twine,   the brave    with en - - - - -

en - - - - -

en - - - - -

glo - ry's wreath en - twine, the brave with glo - ry's wreath en -

glo - ry's wreath en - twine, the brave with glo - ry's wreath en -

en - - - - -

glo - ry's wreath en - twine, the brave with glo - ry's wreath en -

glo - ry's wreath en - twine, the brave with glo - ry's wreath en -

- twine !      oh, hap - py mo - ment,...      a - way all sor - row,..... hence sighs and

- twine !      oh, hap - py mo - ment,...... a - way all sor - row,...... hence sighs and

- twine !      oh, hap - py mo - ment,...... a - way all sor - row,...... hence sighs and

- twine !      oh, hap - py mo - ment,...... a - way all sor - row,...... hence sighs and

- twine !      oh, hap - py mo - - ment,

- twine !      oh, hap - py mo - ment,...... a - way all sor - row,...... hence sighs and

- twine !      oh, hap - py mo - - ment,

- twine !      oh, hap - py mo - - ment,

The Royal Edition. — "The Siege of Rochelle." — (269)

tear - drops...... un - til to - mor - row, joy's gold-en trans - ports,...... oh, let us

tear - drops...... un - til to - mor - row, joy's gold-en trans - ports,...... oh, let us

tear - drops...... un - til to - mor - row, joy's gold-en trans - ports,...... oh, let us

tear - drops...... un - til to - mor - row, joy's gold-en trans - ports,...... oh, let us

a - way all sor - - row, joy's gold-en trans - -

tear - drops...... un - til to - mor - row, joy's gold-en trans - ports,...... oh, let us

a - way all sor - - row, joy's gold-en trans - -

a - way all sor - - row, joy's gold-en trans - -

bor - row...... while yet the sun of........... rap-ture shine, each past re -

bor - row...... while yet the sun of........... rap-ture shine, each past re -

bor - row...... while yet the sun of........... rap-ture shine, each past re -

bor - row...... while yet the sun of........... rap-ture shine,

- ports, oh, let us bor - - row,

bor - row...... while yet the sun of........... rap-ture shine, each past re -

- ports, oh, let us bor - - row

- ports, oh, let us bor - - row,

-gret thus.... for ev - er end - ing,.. ... fame's daz- zling lus - tre...... a - round de -

-gret thus.... for ev - er end - ing,...... fame's daz- zling lus - tre...... a - round de -

-gret thus.... for ev - er end - ing,...... fame's daz- zling lus - tre...... a - round de -

each past re - gret for ev - er end - -

each past re - gret for ev - er end - -

-gret thus.... for ev - er end - ing,...... fame's daz- zling lus - tre...... a - round de -

each past re - gret for ev - er end - -

each past re - gret for ev - er end - -

-scend - ing, fame's daz-zling lus-tre a - round de - scend - ing, de - scend - ing

-scend - ing, fame's daz-zling lus-tre a - round de - scend - ing, de - scend - ing,

-scend - ing, fame's daz-zling lus-tre a - round de - scend - ing, de - scend - ing,

- ing, fame's daz - zling lus-tre a - round de - scend - ing, de - scend - ing,

- ing, for ev - - er,

- scend - ing, de - scend - ing,

- ing, for ev - - er,

- ing, for ev - - er,

vic - to - ry    al - so........ her bright aid  lend - ing,...... the brave with glo - ry's.....

vic - to - ry    al - so........ her bright aid  lend - ing,...... the brave with glo - ry's.....

vic - to - ry    al - so........ her bright aid  lend - ing,...... the brave with glo - ry's.....

vic - to - ry    al - so........ her bright aid  lend - ing,...... the brave with glo - ry's.....

vic - to - ry    al - so........ her bright aid  lend - ing,...... the brave with glo - ry's.....

vic - to - ry    al - so........ her bright aid  lend - ing,...... the brave with glo - ry's.....

vic - to - ry    al - so........ her bright aid  lend - ing,...... the brave with glo - ry's.....

vic - to - ry    al - so........ her bright aid  lend - ing,...... the brave with glo - ry's.....

ff

...... wreath en - twine, the brave with glo - ry's wreath, with glo - ry's

...... wreath en - twine, the brave with glo - ry's wreath, with glo - ry's

...... wreath en - twine, the brave with glo - ry's wreath, with glo - ry's

...... wreath en - twine, the brave with glo - ry's wreath, with glo - ry's

...... wreath en - twine, the brave with glo - ry's wreath, with glo - ry's

...... wreath en - twine, the brave with glo - ry's wreath, with glo - ry's

...... wreath en - twine, the brave with glo - ry's wreath, with glo - ry's

...... wreath en - twine, the brave with glo - ry's wreath, with glo - ry's wreath en - twine, yes, en - - twine,

wreath en - twine, yes, en - - twine,

wreath en - twine, yes, en - - twine,

wreath en - twine, with glo - ry's wreath en - - twine,

wreath en - twine, with glo - ry's wreath en - - twine,

wreath en - twine, yes, en - - twine,

wreath en - twine, yes, en - - twine,

wreath en - twine, with glo - ry's wreath en - - twine,

with glo - - ry's wreath en - twine, with

with glo - - ry's wreath en - twine, with

with glo - - ry's wreath en - twine, with

with glo - - ry's wreath en - twine, with

with glo - - ry's wreath en - twine, with

with glo - - ry's wreath en - twine, with

with glo - - ry's wreath en - twine, with

with glo - - ry's wreath en - twine, with

glo - ry's wreath       the       brave       en - - twine, yes,....

glo - ry's wreath       the       brave       en - - twine, yes,....

glo - ry's wreath       the       brave       en - - twine, yes,....

glo - ry's wreath       the       brave       en - - twine, yes,....

glo - ry's wreath       the       brave       en - - twine, yes,....

glo - ry's wreath       the       brave       en - - twine, yes,....

glo - ry's wreath       the       brave       en - - twine, yes,....

glo - ry's wreath       the       brave       en - - twine, yes,....

.... with glo - ry's wreath en - twine, yes,........ with glo - ry's

.... with glo - ry's wreath en - twine, yes,........ with glo - ry's

. .... with glo - ry's wreath en - twine, yes,........ with glo - ry's

.... with glo - - ry's wreath, yes,..... with glo -

.... with glo - - ry's wreath, yes,..... with glo -

.... with glo - - ry's wreath, yes,..... with glo -

.... with glo - - ry's wreath, yes,..... with glo -

.... with glo - - ry's wreath, yes,..... with glo -

wreath en-twine, en-twine the brave, en-twine the brave.

wreath en-twine, en-twine the brave, en-twine the brave.

wreath en-twine, en-twine the brave, en-twine the brave.

-ry's wreath en-twine the brave, en-twine the brave.

-ry's wreath en-twine the brave, en-twine the brave.

-ry's wreath en-twine the brave, en-twine the brave.

-ry's wreath en-twine the brave, en-twine the brave.

-ry's wreath en-twine the brave, en-twine the brave.

END OF OPERA.

www.ingramcontent.com/pod-product-compliance
Lightning Source LLC
Chambersburg PA
CBHW030337270326
41926CB00009B/864